MY BOOK

𝕷 LUCILLE

𝕷 LAWSON

Flowers of Evil

Charles Baudelaire

FLOWERS OF EVIL

*Translated into English verse
by various hands. Edited, with an
introduction and notes, by* JAMES LAVER
*and illustrated with engravings
by* PIERRE-YVES TRÉMOIS

THE HERITAGE PRESS, NEW YORK

CONTENTS

THE ENGRAVINGS

(The roman numerals are those of the poems illustrated;
the English is from the corresponding lines of the versions printed in this volume.)

INTRODUCTION

BAUDELAIRE was fond of attributing part at least of the strangeness of his character to the ill-assorted ages of his parents when they were married. With his habitual exaggeration he suggested that his father was already in the seventies; actually he was sixty-two and his bride was twenty-eight, and to her, no less than to her son, Joseph François Baudelaire must have seemed like a survivor from another epoch.

The old man had been born in Champagne in 1759. He came of peasant stock, but his parents seem to have enjoyed a certain comfort and they gave their son an excellent education, so good an education that he was able to accept a post as tutor in the family of the Duc de Choiseul-Praslin. In such a household the post of tutor was by no means a servile one. Joseph François Baudelaire seems to have had a house of his own in which he lived with his pupils, and to have received his master and mistress at dinner when occasion arose.

Naturally enough, perhaps, in that enlightened milieu, he professed mildly revolutionary views and was a friend of Condorcet and Helvetius; but when the Revolution came, he soon grew tired of its excesses and exerted himself successfully in saving the life of his old patron. He was rewarded, when the revolutionary flood had subsided, with an administrative post in the Senate and was, when the new century dawned, a man of some position and substance. His first wife died in 1814, leaving behind her one son, who afterwards became a magistrate but of whom little else is known.

One of the houses which François Baudelaire was in the habit of visiting was that of a certain Pierre Perignon, and here he found a young woman in the ambiguous and semi-servile condition of companion to the rich bourgeois' daughters. She was of better family than they, being in fact the daughter of a Royalist officer who, with his wife and unborn child, had fled from Paris during the worst days of the Terror. It was for that reason that Caroline Archimbaut-

Dufays had been born in London and baptised at St. Pancras. But the France of Napoleon was no more likely to forward the career of a Royalist officer than the France of Robespierre, and Mademoiselle Archimbaut-Dufays, as a young woman of twenty-one, had been taken in by the Perignons out of charity.

Although not beautiful, she had a melancholy charm and grace which attracted the attention of François Baudelaire. The young men who came to the house may have noticed it too, but they had obviously no intention of marrying a girl without a *dot*. The old gentleman waited until 1819, when she was in her twenty-sixth year, and when there must have seemed no future before her but that of the dependent old maid. Then he proposed to her, and she accepted him.

That she was not in love with her elderly husband appears obvious enough. She seems to have regarded him with a mixture of affection and awe and to have been more than a little embarrassed by his *ancien régime* gallantry. But she was pious, submissive, devoted and, we may well believe, grateful, and on April 9th, 1821, she crowned the old man's happiness by presenting him with a son, who was baptised with the names of Charles Pierre.

François Baudelaire was immensely proud of the child of his old age. He taught the boy to read, placed before him his own collection of engravings after the best pictures and made it a pleasure to walk with his son through the gardens of the Luxembourg and to point out to him the beauty of the statues. Much of the future poet's enthusiasm for the arts, his apparently instinctive knowledge of good and bad in painting and his passion for 'images' must be traced to his father's influence. But this influence was not to be long continued, for when the boy was five years old his father died.

Charles was left in the hands of his mother and the old nurse Mariette, for whom he had an abiding affection, celebrated in later life in the beautiful poem, *La servante au grand cœur*. The next few years were to have a profound effect upon his sensibility, always morbidly acute. He was bathed, as it were, in an atmosphere of femininity, at once sweet and all enveloping, and in his case it is no exaggeration to say that he was precociously conscious even of the seduction of woman, of the mysteries of her toilet, of the voluptuousness of furs and scents and rustling garments.

This period Baudelaire was afterwards to look back upon as the happiest of his life. The two women and the boy lived together in the closest intimacy. They had moved, for reasons of economy, from the house in the Rue Hautefeuille where the Librairie Hachette now stands, to a smaller house, and then to one still smaller in the Rue du Bac. They had also a little house in the country at Neuilly, and here the over-sensitive child spent delicious hours, dreaming in the little garden, with its dilapidated statues, served silently by Mariette as he took his meals with his mother, and spending long evenings poring over his books in the company of the two women.

But soon another influence was to shatter this idyll. Near the house in the Rue du Bac lived a handsome soldier named Aupick. From neighbours he and Madame Baudelaire became friends. He took to visiting the house, and in 1828—two years after the death of François Baudelaire—he asked the young and still attractive widow to be his wife. To the rage and grief of her son, she consented, and the young child found himself a member now of a very different household, a household of which he was no longer the centre, ruled over by an alien and authoritative presence. That Aupick was a man of upright and admirable character and did his best to win both the affection and the respect of his stepson, made no difference. His being there at all was an unpardonable outrage in the eyes of the precocious child.

The psycho-analysts have pushed their studies of Baudelaire's character to extravagant lengths: some of them will not even allow the poet to mention the sea without concluding that he was really thinking of his mother; but it must be confessed that Baudelaire provides the perfect case-history for their favourite hypothesis. He already adored his mother with a passion which, if it be not inevitable between all mothers and all sons, as the psycho-analysts say, was at least sufficiently potent with him. Circumstances almost compelled him to hate and be jealous of his new father, and the very successes of that father and his wife's obvious love and admiration for him, only made the wound the deeper.

The marriage took place in November, 1828. Caroline was thirty-five, Aupick not yet forty. Soon afterwards the death of Mariette severed the last link which bound Baudelaire to the childish woman-guarded life he had loved so well. Even the familiar surroundings were changed for others less congenial, for, four years after the marriage, when Charles was eleven years old, the family moved to Lyons, where Aupick had received a high military post. It was necessary to provide for the boy's education and Charles was sent to the Collège Royal. Perhaps because Aupick genuinely desired to make him more manly, or perhaps because his presence in the household was an increasing strain, he became a boarder in the establishment, although his own home was only a short distance away. It was another grievance against the hated stepfather.

In 1836 Aupick was recalled to Paris, and Baudelaire, now aged fifteen, was sent to Louis-le-Grand, one of the most famous schools in the capital. His intellectual powers were beginning to expand. He was a moody and difficult pupil, but of his capacity there could be no doubt, and he seems to have been more mature than most boys of his age even in France. He read voraciously, absorbed Victor Hugo and Gautier, read *René* and came under the then universal influence of Chateaubriand. He read Diderot's *La Religieuse*, but his real passion was Sainte-Beuve, especially those early works, *Joseph Delorme* and *Volupté*, which in their blend of sensitiveness and eroticism were likely to be highly dangerous to an impressionable youth. 'Sainte-Beuve is my vice,' he said in later years.

This part of his history is sufficiently obscure. From a hint dropped by the poet himself it seems plain that he had a religious crisis of some kind; but if so, it quickly passed. He became known among his fellows and his teachers for the outrageous cynicism of his opinions, and for these, or for some more serious reason, he was, in 1839, expelled from the Collège. It was obvious that he had no intention of becoming the industrious and dutiful son for which Aupick and his mother hoped.

Aupick was now a man of considerable influence: he had been promoted to the rank of General, and it would have been easy for him to push his stepson in the diplomatic career. Baudelaire, however, had no intention of turning his stepfather's position to advantage. He had decided to take up literature, and this is a decision which never causes any great joy in prosperous and conservative households. None the less, an effort was made to help him, and it was decided that he should be placed in a *pension* with a tutor while he prepared for his degree. The choice fell upon the Pension Bailly in the Rue de l'Estrapade in the Quartier Latin. This was a respectable house frequented by boys of good family and ruled over by the editor of the paper *l'Univers*; but the life which was lived there naturally gave Baudelaire very much more liberty than he had enjoyed at college, and he was not slow to take advantage of it.

He found himself one of a group of young men, nearly all of whom had literary ambitions, and who were all fervent admirers of the Romantics. Charles already wore his Romanticism with a difference — the outward semblance of Romanticism, its mantle of grandiloquence, its shaggy-bearded eccentricity, always repelled him. He was not content, as they were, that Romanticism should be simply an attitude. He took it seriously and determined to discover in his own person the utmost limits to which sensibility could be pushed. In his own way he regarded himself even at this early age as a dedicated soul: perhaps it would be more intelligible to say, as a 'lost' soul, for the course which Baudelaire had mapped out for himself involved throwing over every prejudice, overcoming every repugnance and the resolute exploration of the furthest and lowest reaches of the human soul. For such a programme, the mastery of self was a first requirement, and Baudelaire's mastery of self took the form of an extreme dandyism.

Many writers have commented upon and tried to explain this dandyism of Baudelaire. He has been called a 'dandy lost among the Bohemians,' a mixture of Byron and Brummel. Certainly, his dandyism, like his Romanticism, had its own peculiar qualities. He was not by nature sociable. In fact, we have every reason to believe that he always found himself somewhat ill at ease in polite society. Yet his coat was carefully, even too carefully, tailored. His cravat was elaborately tied, and his linen—even in his days of misery and destitution—was always immaculate. His manners matched his garments. Where his friends were extravagant, bold-voiced, full of practical jokes in the true tradition of *la Bohème*, he was scrupulously, even excessively, polite as if in memory of the *ancien régime* manners of his father, and he only sought to astonish by the unexpectedness of his remarks and the cynicism of his attitude.

Prarond, one of his comrades at the Pension Bailly, is our authority for the fact that he had already written some of the most characteristic poems of the *Fleurs du Mal*. A few of them appeared in the ultra-Romantic review, *Le Corsaire*, and he was already beginning to be known in the world of letters as a young writer of promise. He made the acquaintance of such established figures as Gérard de Nerval, Balzac and Leconte de Lisle, who encouraged him and took him seriously.

That was one side of the *vie de Bohème*, but there was another side into which Baudelaire plunged with equal, or even greater, enthusiasm. In the company of a certain Privat d'Anglemont, who was afterwards to write a book on *Unknown Paris*, he explored the cafés, the cabarets and the houses of prostitution in the Quartier Latin and farther afield.

It was during one of these explorations that he fell in with Sarah, the girl he called 'Louchette' because she squinted. The 'frightful Jewess' inspired one of his most sinister and celebrated poems, and it was probably from her that he contracted syphilis, the disease which was to pursue him for the rest of his life. At all events, he did contract it, and one can only imagine the terrible scene which took place at home when he was compelled to confess his condition to his step-father and his mother. So these were the results of taking up litera-ture instead of adopting an honourable profession like diplomacy, as the General wished! In an effort to rescue Charles from the cesspool into which he had fallen, and to do something to restore his health, it was decided to send him on a long voyage. But before this could be arranged there were more storms in the Aupick household.

Baudelaire sometimes found himself compelled to attend the large and formal dinner-parties given by the General to his colleagues and their wives. On one such occasion, when relations were particularly strained between stepfather and stepson, the latter indulged at table in a series of his usual outrageously cynical remarks. At last the Gen-eral could bear it no longer. He reproved the young man sharply before all the guests and Baudelaire, bounding to his feet, announced with an icy but ferocious politeness that it was his firm intention to strangle him. Perhaps he thought that he would provoke Aupick to a duel, but the General, magnificent in his uniform, merely rose to his feet and administered a sound box on the ear to the enraged young man. Baudelaire fell to the floor in a paroxysm of rage and humiliation and was carried away by the servants. It was plain that this state of things could not go on. The sooner he left for some dis-tant country the better for all concerned, and in May, 1841, he em-barked at Gravelines in *Le Paquebot des Mers du Sud*, bound for Calcutta via the Cape of Good Hope.

There was no hardship in this voyage. Baudelaire was a passenger, and he had been commended to the particular care of the worthy Captain Saur, but he bitterly resented being torn away from his be-loved Paris. He regarded the voyage as an exile imposed on him by the hated authority of his stepfather, and his behaviour on board, among the other passengers, soon made it plain that he intended to make himself as disagreeable as possible.

Saur, who had been instructed to send home reports to the Gen-eral, could not understand the young man who had been entrusted to his charge. He was so obviously cultivated; he had the manners of a gentleman and could be, when he wished, charming and amusing. In the tempest which fell upon the ship as it rounded the Cape of

Good Hope he showed himself full of courage. Yet he seemed for most of the time to be possessed by a black demon and weighed down by an incurable melancholy. For the conversation of his fellow-passengers, for the innocent diversions of shipboard, he made it plain that he had no taste whatever. He did not even seem to have any interest in the romantic land which he was going to see when the ship reached her destination.

The vessel had suffered so severely in the storm that the captain was compelled to put in to Port Louis in the island of Mauritius to re-fit. The passengers disembarked and put up at an hotel, but Baudelaire had little taste for their company and would have been entirely solitary if he had not made some acquaintances in the small French society of the place. He found among them a number of people with an interest in letters and although, from his point of view, they were sadly out of date and had hardly even heard of Romanticism, he seems to have taken pleasure in the society or, at least, in the house of a certain M. Armand de Bragard who had the additional advantage of possessing a very beautiful wife.

Nothing is more characteristic of Baudelaire than his behaviour with regard to this lady. He, who had plunged into the lowest strata of Parisian life and was, by most standards, already something of a debauchee, treated the wife of his friend with scrupulous correctness. He was no Byron, no Lovelace, no Don Juan, no *séducteur*—amateur or professional. Indeed, part of his preference for the prostitute must be set down to his ineradicable timidity in the presence of respectable women. It seems certain that he admired Mme. Armand de Bragard, but when at the next port-of-call he despatched to her some complimentary verses, he was careful to send them through her husband with an explanatory letter. This was the poem entitled, *A une dame créole*, and there was nothing in it to which any husband could possibly take exception.

After three weeks at Port Louis, Baudelaire set sail again, but it was found necessary to put in at St. Denis in the Isle Bourbon for a further twenty-six days, and it was here that he decided to endure his exile from Paris no longer. The Captain tried to dissuade him from his project of returning home, but it may well be believed that he was not at all sorry to see the last of his difficult passenger. In any case, Baudelaire, abandoning the plan of going to India, embarked in another vessel and landed at Bordeaux at the beginning of February, 1842, after nine months' travel. Restless and unhappy, he spent another two months at home and then, on April 9th, 1842, the day

on which he attained his majority, he put his few belongings together and, without saying a word to anyone, left the General's
house for ever.

He was now in possession of the small patrimony left him by his
father and he proceeded to plunge once more into the life of Paris.
But he had done with the Pension Bailly, few as its restrictions had
been, and was determined henceforward to lead the life of a dandy
and man of letters in the manner which suited him best.

He took a small room — the magnificence of this abode has been
much exaggerated — in the Hotel Pimodan on the Quai d'Anjou,
one of the old aristocratic houses on the Ile Saint-Louis, now let out
into apartments and much frequented by the wealthier young Romantics. In one of the larger rooms of the same house took place the
meetings of the Club des Hachischins, a group of young men who
met to stimulate their imaginations by a new oriental vice, hoping
to find the enlargement of their sensibilities and the sharpening of
their talents in the fumes of the Indian hemp. It was here Théophile
Gautier first met the young Baudelaire and he has left a memorable
description of his appearance at this time of life.

'His aspect was striking. His beautiful black hair, cut very close in
regular points over the startlingly white forehead, looked like a kind
of saracen casque. His eyes, the colour of Spanish tobacco, were both
witty and profound with a perhaps too insistent penetration. The
mouth, furnished with very white teeth, showed under a light silky
moustache shading its contour lines, voluptuous and ironical as the
lips of figures painted by Leonardo da Vinci. The nose, fine and
delicate, somewhat rounded with quivering nostrils, seemed to sniff
vague, far-away perfumes. A deep cleft accentuated the chin like the
sculptor's final *coup de pouce*. The cheeks, carefully shaved, bluish and
powdered, contrasted with the vermilion shade of the cheekbones.
The neck, of feminine whiteness and elegance, emerged from a white
turned-down shirt collar and a narrow check tie of Indian stuff. His
clothes consisted of a frock coat of a shiny black material, nut-coloured
trousers, white socks and varnished pumps, the whole meticulously
clean and correct, with a deliberate air of English simplicity.'

The strange thing was that now he was back in Paris he found that
his voyage had left in him a curious nostalgia for blue skies, palm
trees, the brightness of sunlit houses, the hard edge of shadows: most
of all, for the brown bodies of the native girls he had seen at Mauritius and the Isle Bourbon. Their suppleness, their grace, their animal
innocence had attracted him strongly, and it is possible that he had

actually had relations with *la belle Dorothée*, who was the foster-sister of Mme. Armand de Bragard and a servant in her household. That Baudelaire's own attitude towards native women was perverse and, indeed, pathological, may be judged from the profound impression which had been made upon him by seeing a Negress whipped in a public square in Mauritius. Be that as it may, almost his first action on returning to Paris was to take as his mistress a quadroon or octo-roon. This was Jeanne Duval, the Black Venus who was to play such an important, and indeed preponderating, part in his life both as a man and a poet.

Nadar, one of the pioneers of photography, and a friend of many famous figures of the Romantic Movement, relates that, being taken with the grace, if not the talent, of a coloured actress in the little theatre of the Panthéon, he sought her acquaintance and was invited back to her apartment. He found, apparently to his surprise, that the woman had a lover, although she did not seem to take this lover very seriously, for she informed Nadar that he was welcome to come any time except between two and four, which was *l'heure de Monsieur*. Jeanne Duval, for such it was, had a blonde and white-skinned maid and it was borne in upon Nadar that the love-making of Monsieur was not exempt from phantasy. The monsieur in question, it is per-haps needless to add, was Baudelaire himself. Baudelaire, in fact, as a result of his upbringing, his timidity, his malady and the excessively cerebral nature of his emotional excitement, had succeeded in realis-ing that divorce between love and the physical act which is the basis of all the perversions of eroticism. Incapable or almost incapable of all normal gratification, he was henceforth condemned to descend ever deeper and deeper into the infernal spiral which leads to prostra-tion of body, exasperation of nerves and the Dark Night of the Soul.

Left to herself, Jeanne Duval, led by the imperious desires of her own blood with its strong Negro admixture, might have lived a simple and comparatively innocent life on the borders of Parisian prostitution. Goaded by Baudelaire and goading him in her turn, she descended with him into the hell which his imagination created. Let us not forget, however, that from this hell there came forth — like a voice from the Pit — some of the profoundest accents in the whole history of poetry. If it were not so, the name of Baudelaire would long since have been lost in the slime which almost covered him, and his biography, save perhaps as a paragraph in the case-book of an alienist, would never have been written.

While Baudelaire continued to live at the Hotel Pimodan, Jeanne

had an apartment of her own, but his connection with her, and perhaps other liaisons of which we know nothing, soon began to make
large holes in the modest 75,000 francs bequeathed him by his father.
Thirty thousand francs had gone already, and he had begun to ad-
dress to his mother those persistent appeals for money which were,
unfortunately, to continue all his life. The family took alarm, and in
1844, only two years after his majority, a *conseil judiciaire* was imposed upon him and he was given a certain M. Ancelle as his legal
guardian. From what remained of his fortune, he was allowed 200
francs a month.

His rage may be imagined. Even before the imposition of legal
restrictions on his expenditure, the vagabond existence, the constant
flight from creditors had already begun. It has been estimated that
between 1842 and 1858 he changed his lodging some fifteen times.
Sometimes he would present himself at the houses of friends and stay
with them for one, two, or many nights; sometimes he disappeared
altogether in the Paris which he had made his own. He became a
wanderer. Yet, strangely enough, this was the most productive period of his life, and productive not only of poetry. His commentary
on the Salon of 1845 inaugurated the series which make him, in
retrospect at least, the most distinguished and penetrating art-critic
of the nineteenth century.

It is not the place here to discuss his contributions to aesthetics; it
is enough to place him by the side of a critic of the eminence of
Ruskin, for example, to see how astonishingly sound were his re-
actions to contemporary painters, and how often his judgments have
been endorsed by posterity. He was the consistent champion of the
great Delacroix; he was the discoverer of Constantin Guys; he sup-
ported Manet when that revolutionary painter was not the old master
he has since become, but a young revolutionary whose innovations
were regarded by the leaders of French thought as not only senseless
but immoral. In music he was one of the first Frenchmen to salute
the genius of Wagner. His feeling for literature was equally sound,
not only for French writers, but for foreigners. He was the creator
of the European reputation of Edgar Allan Poe.

Poe, indeed, became for him a kind of second self. It was in 1846
that the work of the great American was first brought to his notice,
and Baudelaire was so much struck by the resemblance between
Poe's career and his own that he determined to give a translation of
his works to the French public. He took endless pains to perfect the
English which he had learnt from his mother, and his translation of

the tales of Poe is a supreme example of how closely a foreign language can be made to follow the thoughts of an author. Baudelaire's prose fits Edgar Allan Poe like a glove.

Suddenly there burst upon the Paris of Baudelaire the Revolution of 1848, and the poet's part in it is so paradoxical that it needs to be examined in some detail. Almost the whole of literary Paris was against Louis Philippe. Authors and artists left their desks and their studios and swarmed into the streets, manned the barricades, pillaged weapons from the gun shops. Their unanimity was a spontaneous protest against the growing tyranny of the rising bourgeoisie. This feeling at least Baudelaire shared, and for a moment he seemed to be sufficiently carried away by the prevailing tide of sentiment to imagine that he shared also the revolutionary ideals of his friends. Yet the whole tenor of his life was in opposition to the liberal optimism which derived ultimately from Jean Jacques Rousseau, a writer for whom Baudelaire had nothing but the most blistering contempt. His instincts were aristocratic and pessimistic. In later years, he professed to think that the only pleasure he had found in joining the revolutionary movement was the pleasure of doing evil with his eyes open. At the time he behaved like everybody else, but even in the midst of the turmoil his conduct had that touch of the personal and the eccentric which characterised all his actions. The crowd howled for the overthrow of the King — Baudelaire cried, 'Let us go and shoot General Aupick!' Fortunately, so bloodthirsty a proposal was not put into effect. Instead, Baudelaire's stepfather was one of the beneficiaries of the Revolution of 1848, for Lamartine, who admired him, made him Ambassador at Constantinople.

The political upheaval had thrown Baudelaire into journalism, and for a time he seems to have thought quite seriously of trying to support himself by political writing. In collaboration with two of his friends, Champfleury and Toubin, he founded a republican sheet, *Le Salut Public*, which expired after the publication of two numbers. In 1849 he accepted a post on a paper at Dijon, but the return of his malady put an end to this project also. He returned to Paris, discouraged, and completely altered in appearance, for it was at this period that he shaved his beard and adopted that appearance of the unfrocked priest which he kept for the rest of his life. He was just thirty, but he looked much older.

Early in the '50's, he made another attempt to establish himself in journalism and accepted a post as editor of a paper at Châteauroux. Characteristically, he took an actress with him on the journey and introduced her to the local notables as his wife. This action, and the cynical violence of his opinions, soon led to the termination of his appointment, and he returned once more to Paris.

Now occurred one of the strangest episodes in Baudelaire's career. Humiliated in his body by the growing ravages of his malady, distressed by the non-recognition of his powers, and weary of the burden which Jeanne Duval had now become for him, it was as if he looked round the world for some other kind of love, a love in which there was at least a chance of finding an ideal element. Baudelaire, in short, had a deep spiritual need of a woman he could respect and his choice fell upon a certain Aglaë Savatier, who called herself Madame Sabatier, and was known to all her friends as *La Présidente*. She was to represent the good woman in his life as Jeanne Duval represented the bad. She was to be his ideal, his guiding star, and to rescue him from the abyss into which he had fallen.

The choice was a sufficiently strange one. Madame Sabatier was a woman of abounding vitality, good humour, excellent heart and very easy morals. She was the official mistress of the banker, Mosselmann, but she was also known to have been more than kind to Clésinger, the sculptor, Meissonnier the painter, and Théophile Gautier, who had addressed to her some famous and somewhat obscene letters. Some time previously, while he was still on the Ile Saint-Louis, Baudelaire had met her in the Club des Hachischins. He could therefore have been under no illusion. Nevertheless, she seemed to him, by contrast with most of the women he had known, a positive angel of light. For five years, between 1852 and 1857, he sent her a series of letters and verses.

It is characteristic of his timidity in the face of what he regarded as a respectable woman, that these were all written in a disguised hand. The lady's curiosity was piqued and she was not long in discovering the source of these complimentary messages; but for a long time Baudelaire continued to send them to her without making any further advance. He was content to admire from a distance, and to express his feelings in poetry. The so-called *Cycle de Madame Sabatier* forms an important part of the poetical output of Baudelaire and includes some of his finest verses.

It would perhaps have been better if matters had remained at this point, but Madame Sabatier was too good-natured to resist even such veiled advances as these and she made few difficulties about becoming his mistress. The result was disastrous. It has been suggested that Baudelaire found himself physically incapable of taking advantage of the opportunity. In any case, the fact that she was willing to offer herself robbed Madame Sabatier in his eyes of all prestige. Immediately the poems take on a very different tone. It says much for the good-nature of *La Présidente* that she forgave him and remained his friend till the end of his life.

Meanwhile Baudelaire's reputation as a poet was steadily growing, at least in a limited circle. Eighteen of his poems were published in 1855 in the *Revue des Deux-Mondes* and he began to think seriously about bringing out his best work in a volume. He had had enough verses for such a project for the last ten or twelve years; but Baudelaire, so apparently irregular and lethargic in his life, was a man of scrupulous integrity as an artist. He polished his verses incessantly, strove to eliminate any unsatisfactory epithet, took immense pains to substitute for an image that would have satisfied almost any other poet, one yet more vivid and striking. He was a master of language and a master of the subtler shades of prosody. Pedantic critics might find his verses incorrect; posterity has recognised in him a writer almost impeccable.

The publication of some of the poems in the *Revue des Deux-Mondes* did Baudelaire at the moment more harm than good. They caused such a scandal, both by the daring of their treatment and the nature of the subjects chosen, that editors showed themselves not unaccountably shy of publishing the entire *œuvre*. In the end, Baudelaire was compelled to have recourse to a publisher of Alençon, Auguste Poulet-Malassis by name, a man who had been so deeply involved in the Revolution of 1848 that he had been sentenced to transportation. He had returned, however, to his native town and become the printer of the local paper. He had a passion for poetry, had already brought out the verses of Théodore de Banville, and in 1856 he agreed to publish the volume which was to be known as *Les Fleurs du Mal*. A hundred times the project almost came to nothing. Baudelaire was forever suggesting alterations, re-writing whole lines, correcting and re-correcting proofs. But at last, in the month of July, 1857, the volume was offered to the public.

The outcry was immediate and resounding. In the *Figaro* and the *Constitutionnel*, Baudelaire saw himself attacked both as poet and man. Articles by Baudelaire's friends replying to these attacks were refused by two other leading journals. Sainte-Beuve, whose support Baudelaire had hoped for, gave it in such a half-hearted manner that it did him more harm than good. Strangely enough, the *Moniteur*, the official journal of the Empire, allowed Thierry to defend *Les*

Fleurs du Mal in its pages. None the less, Baudelaire was cited to appear before the *juge d'instruction* and on August 20th, 1857, the trial proper opened.

The result was not long in doubt, if it ever had been, once the action was started. The ingenious defence of his advocate failed to convince the tribunal and Baudelaire was condemned to pay a fine of 300 francs. Six poems were ordered to be excluded from the book: *Lesbos, Femmes damnées, Les Bijoux, Le Léthé, A celle qui est trop gaie,* and *Les Métamorphoses du vampire.* Many people thought that Baudelaire had got off lightly and by an appeal of the Empress he had his fine reduced by fifty francs. He was, none the less, profoundly discouraged and felt himself horribly alone. In his despair, he turned once more to his mother.

Madame Aupick had just lost her husband and had seen herself reduced, by the death of the General, from a position in Society of some brilliance and wealth, to that of a poor widow ekeing out her meagre resources as best she could. She decided to retire to Honfleur, and Baudelaire thought for a time of joining her there. He actually did so for six months, but the experiment was doomed to failure from the beginning. Baudelaire hoped, perhaps, to find again the mother he had known before Aupick had ever come into her life, the woman whose very presence was an almost physical satisfaction, whose every caress was a *volupté.* He found an old lady still so full of the memory of her dead husband that she had a place set for him opposite her at the dinner table every night. Of the position which her son had come to occupy in the world of letters, she understood nothing. She only knew that he had dragged the name of Baudelaire in the mud. She was much under the influence of the local abbé. The poet, with what object it is hard to see, sent him a copy of the *Fleurs du Mal.* The abbé put it in the fire, and in her heart Madame Aupick was not surprised. With all his talents, why could her son not display them in more legitimate fashion?

None the less, Baudelaire gained something from his six months at Honfleur. Some kind of understanding was arrived at, some kind of relationship re-established. Mother and son read English authors together, and although he now knew English better than she, she was still able to correct his pronunciation, and if the mother strove, without success, to enter into the viewpoint of her son, Baudelaire, on his part, made efforts to re-establish himself in life according to her ideas. He began to dream of paying his debts and working regularly every day. He began to believe in the efficacy of prayer. Even on his return to Paris the same mood — but it was more than a mood — continued. The character of Baudelaire had undergone a change. It would be an exaggeration to say that he was converted in the religious sense of the word; but at least his cynicism had fallen away. Satanism had taken on a new and profounder meaning, a meaning not far removed from the attitude of orthodoxy.

Of Baudelaire's life there is little more to be said. In 1860 appeared his *Paradis Artificiels*, including his translation of De Quincey; in 1861, his Study of Richard Wagner and Tannhäuser, and the second edition of the *Fleurs du Mal*, lacking of course the six poems which had been condemned by the Tribunal. In the same year he offered himself for election to the *Académie Française*, a candidature which does not seem so ridiculous to us as it did to his contemporaries, but which, it is hardly necessary to say, did not succeed. In 1864, he made a disastrous journey to Belgium in the hope of making some money by giving lectures; but the end was not far off, and he knew it. Already, in January, 1860, he had had a seizure which indicated the return of his old malady. Two years later he noted in his diary the famous and terrible sentence, 'To-day, January 23rd, 1862, I had a strange warning. I felt passing over me the wind of the wing of Imbecility.' Another two years passed; then, while visiting a church at Namur, he suddenly fell. 'It is nothing; I slipped,' he said: but his friends knew better. Next day, it was obvious that his brain was affected, and soon after he became paralysed all down the right side. He lost the power of speech. '*Cré nom*' — a commonplace oath — was all he could induce his lips to articulate. He was taken to Brussels, where his mother hastened to meet him, but the doctors decided that her presence excited the patient too much. He was taken back to Paris and installed in a *maison de santé*. Here, on August 31st, 1867, he died, peacefully enough, his mother beside him.

Such, in brief outline, was the career of this strange, unhappy man, and if he were nothing more than that, we might be content to leave him with a shrug of pity or the moralist's warning. But Baudelaire is something much more than a moral warning and very much more than a mere mental case of interest to writers of the psycho-analytical school. He was also the author of the *Fleurs du Mal*, one of the most remarkable volumes of poetry the nineteenth, or any other, century has produced. It is a small volume. By the side of the output of a writer like Hugo, it shrinks into insignificance both in actual volume and in extent of subject-matter. Yet while Hugo, acknowledged classic as he is, has almost no influence on modern poetry or on modern sensibility, from the *Fleurs du Mal,* like a radio-active particle, emanate rays which are still powerful.

To consider why this is so would involve an elaborate study of the whole nature of poetry. Even to attempt it in the barest outline is obviously impossible in a short introductory note. A very few words must suffice. Hugo himself, in a happy phrase, hailed Baudelaire as the creator of a '*frisson nouveau,*' and to do this is no doubt one of the main functions of poetry: to enlarge the borders of sensibility and to explore uncharted regions of the human soul. It is not merely a matter of choosing a new subject, it is not merely the search, dear to minor artists of the past generation, for a 'new sketching ground.' It is a veritable enlargement of the instrument, a new string to the lyre, a stretching of the borders of vision into infra-red and ultra-violet, an extension of the chords of hearing so that the hitherto unattainably shrill or unreachably profound notes become parts of the usable scale.

This is not all. A poet is great by reason of his power of evocation, and this power Baudelaire had in a supreme degree. It is not only a matter of choosing rare and curious words: the error of the 'art for art's sake' school which derived from Baudelaire by misunderstanding him. Just as a painter by the just juxtaposition of tones makes each glow with a brilliance it could never have in isolation, so Baudelaire by the just placing of his words—ordinary words for the most part and in common usage—makes each shine with an interior radiance. Light is reflected from one facet to the other until the whole line shines like a string of jewels.

The exactness of an image is not, as the Realists thought, a mere matter of observation and the accumulating of fact on fact; it is a supreme synthesis of the imagination. A single epithet takes the place of a long descriptive analysis; a single noun conjures up a picture. The strength of Baudelaire lay in the unity of his sensorial apparatus. Some poets are visual, some auditory; some are impervious to odours, some are tone-deaf. We know from Baudelaire's critical writings of his extreme sensitiveness to music, his vast knowledge and appreciation of painting, and we gather from his poems and his other writings a feeling of the hyperaesthesia of his sense of smell. He himself spoke of 'correspondences' and there is no doubt that he was profoundly aware of the relations between sounds and colours and between odours and tactile sensations. Such an equipment enabled him to be always, as it were, at the centre of a sensation, never to experience anything externally, as Gautier did, for example, never to be content with a mere verbalism, as Hugo was too often. He is therefore the least rhetorical of poets and the most penetratingly exact. Not only his actors but his décor is solid, and this perhaps is the explanation of the curious sculptural quality of his work, even when it glows and shimmers with colour. For the paradox of Baudelaire is that while his verses never fail to be intensely alive, the movement is all interior; the outline remains pure and static, so that while he is in manner one of the most romantic poets, he is in form one of the most classic, infinitely more so than those false classics, the *Parnassiens*, who fancied that they were carrying on this tradition.

It is a sign of the universality of Baudelaire that so many writers, of such widely divergent schools, should have acknowledged him as master and showed obvious signs of his influence. Neither the *Parnassiens* nor the *Symbolistes* would have been quite the same without his example, and even men of the calibre of Verlaine and Rimbaud are his obvious spiritual children. So, in another art, is a man like Beardsley; and the modern French school of Catholic writers shows the signs of Baudelairism to a marked degree.

It may seem strange to stress his influence upon Catholic writers, and when it is remembered that even the three rebels mentioned in the last paragraph all died in the arms of the Church, it may well be asked what was Baudelaire's own attitude to Catholicism; how far was he, the resolute explorer of the evil in the human soul, the author of the blasphemous *Denial of Peter,* himself a Catholic?

Barbey d'Aurevilly, at the conclusion of a famous review, offered Baudelaire the alternative of becoming a Catholic or committing suicide. Baudelaire himself received the Last Sacraments before he died, but it may be doubted, in view of the condition of his mind at the time, whether this action on his part, or rather on the part of his friends, and particularly of his mother, has any value as evidence. Yet Baudelaire, expressing his indignation at the action of his mother's friend, the abbé, in throwing *Les Fleurs du Mal* into the fire, expressed himself in the phrase: 'The book starts from a Catholic idea.'

It starts, in short, from the doctrine of Original Sin. There were times, no doubt, when Baudelaire was sufficiently the child of his age to accept its third-generation Rousseauism, and Rousseauism, from which nineteenth-century Liberalism was so largely descended, and which is still the inspiration behind so many humanitarian activities, rests ultimately upon a denial of Original Sin. Man is not only born free — and is now everywhere in chains — but is born good and is now everywhere corrupted, the changes in both cases being due to the badness of social institutions and the villainy of kings and priests. Therefore natural instincts are good; therefore self-expression is good; therefore it is good for man to enlarge his personality to the utmost possible limits. It was this notion which created the heroes and the giants of the Romantic Movement. Baudelaire was a Romantic with a difference, although the difference was not at first perceptible to his contemporaries. Was he not one with them in his contempt for the bourgeois? Did he not join them on the barricades of 1848? He pushed to extravagant lengths their own rebellion against the conventions, against current morality, against the ties of family life. How should it be that he did not share also their belief in the perfectibility of man? Yet even a casual reading of Baudelaire's letters, his remarks to friends and the poems themselves leave no doubt that his dominant belief throughout his life was a belief in the utter and abject natural wickedness of man.

Now, although a belief in Original Sin — at least in its theological form — is not a popular belief or one generally held to-day, it is becoming increasingly obvious to sensitive people, and in particular to creative writers, that the opposite belief has had some unfortunate results. If men's sins are the result of their upbringing and environment, then judgment between good and evil becomes so difficult that it is in practice abandoned. Morality passes over into humanitarianism, and with the loss of belief in a man's absolute responsibility comes also a diminution of his dignity. The old conflict between heaven and hell, of which every man's soul was once the field of battle, becomes strangely unreal, and it does not seem to matter very much what men do or what they leave undone.

In no field are the results of this more obvious than in the field of sexual relationship. If adultery, for example, ceases to be a sin, it ceases to have any meaning and very soon, any interest; and although Baudelaire's own contention that there is no pleasure in sex unless it be accompanied by a sense of sin, is perhaps pathological, it is at least difficult to see from the point of view of the artist how interest can be maintained in the passionless promiscuity of beings whose actions concern only themselves. To put the matter in terms less gravely theological, what has happened is the decay of the tragic sense of life; and to allow the sense of tragedy to decay is to lose the faculty of being, as Aristotle said, 'purged by pity and terror.' Pity becomes merely an exacerbated sensibility and terror the mere fear of losing what comforts and possessions we have. Mankind is forced to fall back on millenarianism, the pathetic belief that Paradise can be established on earth, and that a little more leisure, a little more education, a little more kindness and a few more social services will shortly bring it about. Whether this belief be well founded or not in the social and political sphere, it is fatal to the artist, for it robs him of almost his entire subject-matter.

The defender of Rousseau, the liberal idealist, may well reply: 'What do I care for that? It may be, in the perfect world which is coming, that the artist will be unnecessary. By the progressive abolition of evil we are moving steadily towards a state in which all men will be happy.' Such doctrines cover with a crust of complacency the boiling cauldron of the world; and when, as in present times, the crust shows signs of cracking, and through the fissures come the old authentic flames, the idealist can do no more than lament, with a puzzled anguish, the sudden collapse of all the kindnesses which yesterday were commonplaces, and the slipping back of mankind into barbarism. It is then that a poet like Baudelaire, for all his failures as a man, for all the wilful eccentricity of his behaviour, is seen to have had a clearer grasp of reality than any of the prophets of smooth things.

He was a Romantic, albeit of the second generation, and no doubt he inherited from his forbears certain of their strange properties, some of which go back right into the eighteenth century. There is in him something of the author of the *Castle of Otranto*, something of the Marquis de Sade; there is Byron, Chateaubriand, and even Petrus Borel. His world is a fantastic world of corpses and ghouls, of poisons and fatal passions, but in his hands all these things suddenly become imbued with life. It is as if a conjurer should bring on to the platform the old apparatus with which the public is only too familiar and should suddenly out of a hat produce, not live rabbits, but real demons, and from the end of his wand should spout authentic fire. Or as if a character in a pantomime should disappear through a trapdoor, and as we watch, the trapdoor is no trapdoor but the very lid of Hell. Baudelaire's demons are real, because he found them in his own nature. He set himself to explore every corner of that nature, and if he did so at the cost of his own life and his own reason, that fact alone gives an element of heroism to his action which is not without its grandeur.

'*J'ai cultivé mon hystérie avec jouissance et terreur!*' It is no affectation, this Baudelairism: and even those who are not quite Baudelairian in their outlook may see in him something of the saint, and more than something of the martyr. Only on the most superficial plane is this a paradox. It is a strange fact that although Baudelaire was, by ordinary standards, a debauchee, a pervert, an invalid, and perhaps even a mental case, it is impossible to read his biography, and still more, his poems, without an increased sense of human dignity and a deeper understanding of the tragic meaning of life.

JAMES LAVER

Blackheath, London

A NOTE ON THE TEXT

THE DIFFICULTY of translating poetry into another language is proverbial, and when the creator of such poetry is a writer so delusively simple and so psychologically complex, so rigorous in form and so original in subject-matter as Baudelaire, the difficulty is certainly not diminished. Yet the problem of translating poetry is one which continues to attract the attention and challenge the talents of those who possess two languages and some skill in verse, and the impossibility, or near-impossibility, of success seems to act rather as a spur than as a deterrent. The prose translation is never very satisfactory. To change the language of a poem is no doubt to produce a different work of art, to change the form as well is to produce something on another plane altogether. There is, too, in a mixed collection, a legitimate interest in seeing how the various translators have coped with their task, and how successful they have been, but this is only possible if the original poems are either printed side by side with the translations or are readily accessible in a companion volume. It is the second alternative which has been adopted here.

The editor of the present edition has endeavoured to collect the best obtainable translations of the complete Baudelaire canon as contained in the so-called 'definitive' edition. He decided, after much thought, that this was, after all, the best solution, although it is admitted that the arrangement of the poems is not what Baudelaire would have wished had he lived to see this edition through the press. The difficulty stems from the fact that when the first edition came out in 1857, the Public Prosecutor intervened and banned the book unless certain poems were excluded from it. The *pièces condamnées* numbered six: *Les Bijoux, Le Léthé, A celle qui est trop gaie, Lesbos, Femmes damnées,* and *Les Métamorphoses du vampire.* The second edition appeared in 1861, the banned poems having been removed and thirty-five new poems added. The sections in which the poems were printed were also different.

Baudelaire was planning a third edition which was to contain, in addition to those already published, all the poems he had written between 1863 and 1866. He died in the following year, and the third edition was produced in 1868 by his literary executors, Charles Asselineau and Théodore de Banville.

Their arrangement has been much criticized by later editors, every one of whom has come up with a different solution and a different arrangement, most of them attempting, for example, to fit back into their place the *pièces condamnées,* and to make room for poems not included in the earlier edition. It is obvious that the judgments on which these re-arrangements are based are inevitably subjective and arbitrary. Even Dr. Enid Starkie, who (in her admirable edition) gives the best account of these attempts, is compelled to admit that her own arrangement is not perfect. It is because of all these complications that the present editor has chosen what may be regarded as the easy way out, following the arrangement of the 'definitive' edition and merely adding half-a-dozen poems at the end.

Even so, the task of finding the best English translations was no easy one. In the first place, those who have translated only a few of the poems have very often chosen the same ones. For a poem like *La Vie Antérieure* the editor had the choice of no fewer than seven versions, and of eight for *La Cloche Fêlée.* On the other hand, for some dozen poems no satisfactory translation could then be found at all, for those who have produced 'complete' Baudelaire translations have not worked from the 'definitive' edition. The editor is therefore particularly grateful to Mr. A. Graham Reynolds and Mr. Arthur Ellis, who helped to fill the gaps by preparing new versions. Much help was also given by the latter in his capacity as Librarian at the British Museum and the editor's debt to him is therefore double and gratefully acknowledged. Of the remaining poems — such unrewarding trifles as *L'Amour et le Crâne* and *Une Gravure Fantastique* — the editor was compelled to provide translations himself.

Much use was made of the versions produced a generation ago by Miss Edna St. Vincent Millay and Mr. George Dillon, to whom, and to their heirs (as well as to their publishers, Messrs. Harper & Row) grateful thanks are due. More would have been used but for the present editor's strong conviction that the endeavour to translate the French alexandrine into English hexameter is never wholly satisfactory. As Miss Millay herself points out in her admirable preface, the English twelve-syllable line simply will not behave as a hexameter but breaks into a tetrameter jog-trot, unless it is firmly tied down to a pentameter structure, and becomes either a mere odd line among

Popeian heroic couplets or the long-drawn close of the Spenserian stanza. It is much better when faced with a series of French alexandrines to throw up the sponge, cut the Gordian knot and translate them into English pentameters. Pentameter renderings of alexandrines have therefore been chosen wherever possible.

The reader will perhaps be astonished to find a long extract from Longfellow in the present volume. But Baudelaire did translate a fragment of *Hiawatha*, and as this is included in the text of the French 'definitive' edition it was thought best, for the sake of completeness, to include those lines from Longfellow's poem which correspond to the French version. This will at least enable the reader to compare the two texts with ease and to note the remarkable transformation which the American poet's version underwent at the hands of Baudelaire.

From Sir John Squire's early volume *Poems and Baudelaire Flowers* published in 1909 by the New Age Press, some thirty versions were selected; from James Huneker's *The Poems and Prose Poems of Charles Baudelaire* (Brentano's), twenty versions, including one by Mr. F. P. Sturm; from Mr. Lewis Piaget Shanks' *Les Fleurs du Mal* (published by Messrs. Holt in 1926) eighteen versions. Grateful thanks are due to both authors and publishers for permission to reproduce these, which with the twenty translations by Mr. George Dillon and Miss Edna St. Vincent Millay form the bulk of the volume. Seven versions have been reproduced by kind permission from Mr. Arthur Symons' *Baudelaire* published by the Casanova Society in 1925. It was also a privilege to be able to use the three Baudelaire translations by Lord Alfred Douglas from his *Collected Poems* published by Messrs. Martin Secker. From the same publishers' *Collected Poems of James Elroy Flecker* two admirable versions were culled, and one from Mr. T. Sturge Moore's *Poems* published by Messrs. Macmillan & Co. It was particularly gratifying to be able to reprint Mr. Aldous Huxley's almost incredibly skilful version of *Femmes damnées* from *The Cicadas and Other Poems*, published by Messrs. Chatto & Windus. Other single poems have been collected with grateful thanks from the works of Mr. Arthur Reed Ropes (*Poems*, 1882), Mr. W. J. Robertson (*A Century of French Verse*, 1895), Mr. Countee Cullen (*The Medea and Some Poems*, 1935), Dr. H. W. Garrod (*Poems from the French*, 2nd Series, 1928), Mr. Edward H. Lascelles (*Shadows of the Gods*, 1920), Miss Lois Saunders (*Strangers and Foreigners*, 1912), Miss Margaret Jourdain (*Poems*, 1911), Miss Dorothy Martin (*Sextette*, 1928) and Mr. John Payne (*Flowers of France*, 1906); three trans-

lations from Mr. Cyril Scott's *Baudelaire* published by Messrs. Elkin
Mathews and two by Mr. Harry Curwen. It proved difficult to pro-
cure a copy of Mr. Clark Ashton Smith's *Sandalwood*, 1928, but a
manuscript version of three poems was kindly supplied by Mr.
Edwin Gilcher, who also gave much help, for which the editor is
extremely grateful, by generously making available the ample lists
of Baudelaire translators compiled by his own researches and also
by forwarding a large number of translations in manuscript.

Grateful thanks are due to Mr. Wilfrid Thorley, not only for
much help in the early stages of the project but for allowing the use
of two versions from his *Fleurs de Lys* (published by Messrs. Heine-
mann) and of three unpublished translations. The three translations
from his *Bouquet from France* are reprinted by kind permission of
Messrs. Harrap.

Mr. J. G. Wilson, of Messrs. Bumpus, was most helpful in finding
some necessary books, and as the owner of the copyright of the work
of the late Eugene Mason, he kindly allowed me the use of two
translations from *Flamma Vestalis and Other Poems* published by
Messrs. T. Fisher Unwin.

Lord Derwent generously allowed the inclusion of five of his unpublished versions, and Sir Eric Maclagan three of his. Mr. Humbert
Wolfe, shortly before his untimely death and in spite of enormous
pressure of work, most valiantly produced for the present edition a
special translation of *Le Jeu*.

Gratitude is due also to Mr. Desmond MacCarthy for drawing
attention to several references which might otherwise have been
overlooked.

And finally, the editor wishes to express his thanks to Mr. David
Paul for his permission to use four of his versions in our 'Additional
Poems,' as well as to Mr. Kenneth O. Hanson for allowing the use
of his translation of *Amina Boschetti*.

J. L.

Flowers of Evil

To the Reader

Folly and error, sin and avarice
Lodge in our hearts and work upon our frames;
And like the beggar fattening his lice,
We feed remorse, and call it charming names.

Our sins are tough, our penitence is faint;
We ask fat payment for confession's load,
And thinking our cheap tears will wash the taint,
We gaily turn back to the muddy road.

On evil's pillow Satan Trismegist
Lulls our enchanted soul with patient care,
And by that all-too-learned alchemist,
Our will's metallic worth is blown to air.

The Devil holds our puppet threads! We find
Attraction in things horrible; each day
Through noisome blackness undeterred and blind
To Hell we step yet further on our way.

Like the poor lecher kissing hungrily
An antique wanton's persecuted breast,
We steal a hidden pleasure as we fly,
Pressing it hard as orange-rinds are pressed.

Close-seething tribes of Demons in our brain,
Like millions of worms, hold festival;
And when we breathe, Death with dull sighs of pain
Into our lungs flows down invisible.

If rape and venom, arson and the knife
Have not yet pricked their droll inventions out
On the drab canvas of our pitiful life,
Alas! it is our laggard souls that doubt.

But in our base menagery of vice,
More than the jackals, panthers, bitches, all
The vultures, apes, scorpions and cockatrice,
Monsters that yelp and howl and grunt and crawl,

There's one more cruel, loathsome, hideous yet!
Though he scarce moves, scarce utters, his desire
Is to see ruin where the earth was set,
And swallow in one yawn the world entire;

ENNUI! look how, dreaming a gallows dream,
Half tearfully he smokes his hookah through;
You know this delicate monster, you who seem
My twin, my double – canting reader, you!

[LORD DERWENT]

Spleen and the Ideal

I

Benediction

When by the high decree of powers supreme,
The Poet came into this world outworn,
She who had borne him, in a ghastly dream,
Clenched blasphemous hands at God, and cried in scorn:

'O rather had I borne a writhing knot
Of unclean vipers, than my breast should nurse
This vile derision, of my joy begot
To be my expiation and my curse!

'Since of all women thou hast made of me
Unto my husband a disgust and shame;
Since I may not cast this monstrosity,
Like an old love-epistle, to the flame;

'I will pour out thine overwhelming hate
On this the accursed weapon of thy spite;
This stunted tree I will so desecrate
That not one tainted bud shall see the light!'

So foaming with the foam of hate and shame,
Blind unto God's design inexorable,
With her own hands she fed the purging flame
To crimes maternal consecrate in hell.

Meanwhile beneath an Angel's care unseen
The child disowned grows drunken with the sun;
His food and drink, though they be poor and mean,
With streams of nectar and ambrosia run.

Speaking to clouds and playing with the wind,
With joy he sings the sad Way of the Rood;
His shadowing pilgrim spirit weeps behind
To see him gay as birds are in the wood.

Those he would love looked sideways and with fear,
Or, taking courage from his aspect mild,
Sought who should first bring to his eye the tear,
And spent their anger on the dreaming child.

With all the bread and wine the Poet must eat
They mingled earth and ash and excrement,
All things he touched were spurned beneath their feet;
They mourned if they must tread the road he went.

His wife ran crying in the public square:
'Since he has found me worthy to adore,
Shall I not be as antique idols were,
With gold and with bright colours painted o'er?

'I will be drunk with nard and frankincense,
With myrrh, and knees bowed down, and flesh and wine.
Can I not, smiling, in his love-sick sense,
Usurp the homage due to beings divine?

'I will lay on him my fierce, fragile hand
When I am weary of the impious play;
For well these harpy talons understand
To furrow to his heart their crimson way.

'I'll tear the red thing beating from his breast,
To cast it with disdain upon the ground,
Like a young bird torn trembling from the nest –
His heart shall go to gorge my favourite hound.'

To the far heaven, where gleams a splendid throne,
The Poet uplifts his arms in calm delight,
And the vast beams from his pure spirit flown,
Wrap all the furious peoples from his sight:

'Thou, O my God, be blest who givest pain,
The balm divine for each imperfect heart,
The strong pure essence cleansing every stain
Of sin that keeps us from thy joys apart.

'Among the numbers of thy legions blest,
I know a place awaits the poet there;
Him thou hast bid attend the eternal feast
That Thrones and Virtues and Dominions share.

'I know the one thing noble is a grief
Withstanding earth's and hell's destructive tooth,
And I, through all my dolorous life and brief,
To gain the mystic crown, must cry the truth.

'The jewels lost in Palmyra of old,
Metals unknown, pearls of the outer sea,
Are far too dim to set within the gold
Of the bright crown that Time prepares for me.

'For it is wrought of pure unmingled light,
Dipped in the white flame whence all flame is born –
The flame that makes all eyes, though diamond-bright,
Seem obscure mirrors, darkened and forlorn.'

[JAMES HUNEKER]

II

The Albatross

Often, in sport, a ship's crew love to take
Captive those huge sea-fowl, the albatross,
Whose indolence accompanies her wake
Above the bitter depths she glides across.

They lay them on the deck; and instantly
Cumbrous and shamed, the empyrean's kings
Let trail along their sides distressfully,
Like oars, their once magnificent white wings.

How clumsy the light traveller, how weak,
How hideous-droll, whose beauty shone of late!
One with a cutty-pipe torments his beak,
Another limps, mocking the cripple's fate.

Prince of the clouds, the Poet is like you,
Who ride the storm and laugh at the drawn bow;
Banished on earth amid men's jeers, those two
Gigantic wings forbid his steps to go.

[LORD DERWENT]

III

Elevation

Above the valleys and above the meres,
The mountains and the woods, the clouds, the seas,
Beyond the sun and ether distances,
Beyond the confines of the starry spheres,

Swiftly, my spirit, thou dost hold thy flight,
And, as one swoons with joy on the sea's breast,
Those calm eternal deeps thou furrowest
With an ineffable and strong delight.

Leave far beneath thy feet these pestilent places
To bathe in upper air, and quench desire
With unpolluted draughts of that clear fire
Which fills the luminous and limpid spaces.

O happy who can cast aside his chains,
The heavy load of grief and weariness,
And, winging from this misty wilderness,
Can set his eyes on those far-shining plains!

Whose lark-like thoughts, with bright,
    untrammelled wings,
Spring upward when the morning skies are clear;
Who soars o'er life, and effortless can hear
The secret speech of flowers and dumb things!

[SIR JOHN SQUIRE]

IV

Affinities

Sometimes, in Nature's temple, from the array
Of living columns doubtful murmurs rise;
There Man, watched over by familiar eyes,
Through a thick wood of symbols takes his way.

Like endless echoes mingling at their bounds
In tenebrous, abysmal unity,
Vast as the night and vast as clarity,
Call to each other Perfumes, Colours, Sounds.

Some perfumes like cool children's flesh entice,
Are soft as hautboys, green as meadowland;
Others, triumphal and corrupt with spice,

Having the infinite's power to expand –
Musk, amber, benzoin and frankincense –
Chant the delight of spirit and of sense.

[LORD DERWENT]

V

J'aime le souvenir…

I love to look back to the old, nude days
When Phoebus tinctured statues with gold rays
And man and woman, hindered by no lie
Could carelessly enjoy agility,
Indulging the sane reflex of machines
If the fond sun should stimulate their spines.
Then teeming Cybele was generous,
A she-wolf, she had ample store for us
And with maternal tenderness would hug

THE HERITAGE CLUB

Sandglass

NUMBER XI:36

ISSUED MONTHLY TO THE MEMBERS OF
THE HERITAGE CLUB
AVON, CONNECTICUT 06001

Paradoxical Poet

IN 1864 Charles Baudelaire went to Brussels to lecture on poetry and wrote this note to his publisher:

"Many people crowded, with a booby-like curiosity, about the author of *Les Fleurs du Mal*. The author of the *Flowers* in question could not be otherwise than an unnatural eccentric. All this rabble took me for a monster, and when they saw that I was cold, moderate, and polite—and that I had a horror of freethinkers, progress, and the whole modern idiocy—they decreed (so I imagine) that I *was not the author of my book*. What comic confusion between author and subject! This cursed book (*of which I am very proud*) is, it would seem, very obscure, very unintelligible! I shall bear for a long time the burden of having dared to paint evil with some talent."

When first published in the summer of 1857, *The Flowers of Evil* had been immediately seized by the police. A trial followed and six poems—the six Baude-laire liked best—were suppressed: *The Jewels, Lethe, A Girl Too Gay, Lesbos, Damned Women*, and *Metamorphoses of the Vampire*. If the poet had deliberately set out to *épater les bourgeois* he could not have succeeded better. Yet Baudelaire was shocked and hurt by the uproar that greeted his book.

The paradox is one involving the man and the poet. The man, self-confessed victim of debauchery, drugs, disease, and the debilitating spiritual plague he called "ennui," was doomed from boyhood to a short and painful life. The poet was destined to create a collection of poems which for order, clarity, and beauty have few challengers in the French language. How can these two creatures be reconciled into one Charles Baudelaire? Don't despair if the solution to Baudelaire's mystery eludes you. No one has ever completely answered the riddles posed by the life and work of this remarkable poet.

Though Baudelaire painted evil, he did not celebrate it. Long before it was the fashion to do so, he engaged in an exploration of the dark regions of his own psyche. The flowers he found there were not all pretty, but he gathered them anyway and arranged them in an exotic bouquet which he presented to the world with his characteristic mocking smile.

I

FEW POETS are content with one muse; Charles Baudelaire had many. These were the women, a great variety of them, who endlessly fascinated him and betrayed him, and who provided him with the deepest sources of his poetic inspiration. The list must begin with his mother. Caroline Archimbault Dufays married François Baudelaire, a man of sixty, when she was twenty-six. Charles, their only son, was born in Paris on April 19, 1821; he was five when his father died. Mother and son lived alone together for a few happy years, perhaps the happiest of the poet's life. "What is it," he later wrote, "that a child loves so passionately in his mother . . . ? Is it simply a being who feeds him, combs him, bathes him, and rocks him? It is also the caresses and the sensuous voluptuousness. He loves his mother . . . for the agreeable tickling of satin and fur, for the perfume of her breast and hair, for the clicking of jewels. . . ."

Baudelaire's infant paradise ended abruptly when his mother remarried. Major Aupick meant well by his stepson, but Charles always saw him as a dangerous rival. When he was twenty, after a series of schools which he hated, he was sent on a sea cruise, landing on the isle of Mauritius in the Indian Ocean—a second paradise whose images of exotic flora and fauna and brown native women haunt his later poems.

Back in Paris, the young man, who had begun to write poetry, declined his stepfather's attempts to introduce him to a diplomatic career. On money inherited from his father, he went to live on the Île St. Louis. Baudelaire's biographers sum up the next ten years of his life succinctly—Bohemian life, debts, mistresses. Opium and hashish, they might have added. And Jeanne Duval.

His poetry is full of Jeanne Duval, his "black Venus." Though they never married, when he spoke of *"ma femme"* it was she he spoke of. Theirs was a love-hate relationship, marked for more than twenty years with quarrels, break-ups, and reconciliations.

As he entered his thirties, just about the time he was most immersed in creating *The Flowers of Evil*, Baudelaire began to search for a new sort of muse. He seemed to need an esthetic and emotional contrast to his violent mistress—an unapproachable idol to love from a distance.

There is some irony in his choice. Apollonie Sabatier was already the mistress of another man, and she was well known to be—in the phrase of the day—"generous with her favors." To keep her safely on her pedestal Baudelaire concealed his identity when he sent her the verses she had inspired. But Baudelaire was revealed as their author when *Les Fleurs du Mal* appeared, including the poems later referred to as "the Sabatier cycle." The lady's little sister teased him by asking if he was "in love" with Apollonie. He answered, "Ordinary men are lovers. Poets are idolators."

The last ten years of the poet's life were miserable. In 1860 he suffered the first of a series of strokes which grew steadily worse until, in 1866, he became paralyzed and speechless. Right up to the time of his death on August 31, 1867, his mother, widowed for the second time, took increasing care of him, though she had become devoutly religious and believed that his poems were blasphemous.

Baudelaire devoted his life to poetry, yet produced only one book of poems. The rest of his literary output consists of two volumes of criticism, chiefly of painting; a translation of Thomas de Quincey's *Confessions of an English Opium Eater*; a translation of the tales of Edgar Allan Poe, which possessed a tremendous attraction for him; and a prose piece, *Les Paradis Artificiels*. To his sorrow, Baudelaire's work received little praise or understanding in his lifetime. No one could predict that the young poets such as Rimbaud and Verlaine would turn to him for inspiration rather than to the established masters of the day, or that American and English poets would still feel impelled to translate his fascinating lines.

II

THERE IS ALWAYS a risk in translating poetry, as there is in repotting plants. The plant, or poem, which was getting along beautifully in familiar soil, may not survive the change. Even if it does not die, it may lose all its bloom. So many poets have taken the risk of translating Baudelaire into English that it is now an enormous task to select the best translations. Supremely aware of this fact is James Laver, who prepared the text of *The Flowers of Evil* for us.

Searching for translations that best brought out Baudelaire's jewel-like quality —as well as his stark and strange images— Laver combed British and American publications and studied many renderings of each of the original 158 poems. Eventually, in the work of such poets as Humbert Wolfe, Edna St. Vincent Millay, James Huneker, Lord Alfred Douglas, George Dillon, Arthur Symons, and Sir John Squire, he found exquisite versions of all but one. (That one gave him no trouble whatsoever, as it was a fragment of Longfellow's *Hiawatha* which Baudelaire had translated.)

In our edition you will find the six condemned poems as well as five poems that had not originally appeared in *The Flowers of Evil*. The latter had survived in manuscript, and are now included in order to make our collection complete. Besides his comprehensive introduction, James Laver has provided notes to the poems.

An expert in art, an expert in words, an Englishman for whom French is a second language, James Laver is well qualified to have made some of the translations himself. As an undergraduate at New College, Oxford, he received the Newdigate Prize for poetry. During his long and successful writing career he has contributed lyrics and sketches for London reviews and he has published two collections of his verses, *A Stitch in Time* and *Ladies' Mistakes*. His novel, *Nymph Errant*, was made into a musical comedy by Charles B. Cochran with music by Cole Porter and starred Gertrude Lawrence. His work as a biographer includes lives of Whistler, Wesley, and Huysmans.

In 1922 Laver entered the Victoria and Albert Museum as an Assistant Keeper in the Department of Prints and Drawings, becoming Keeper in 1938. His work in the dating of pictures by a study of the costumes to be found in them led Laver to an interest in the whole complicated field of changing fashion. And so in recent years all of his earlier accomplishments have been overshadowed by his growing fame as a historian of costume and a philosopher of fashion.

His book, *Modesty in Dress*, published in 1969 by Houghton Mifflin, reveals to what extent the wearing of clothes from ancient to modern times has been affected by ego, status, and sexual display more than by the need for protection from the elements.

His expertise in matters of dress has caused Laver to be as highly regarded in the world of fashion as he is in academic circles. He is often asked by the press to comment on such serious upheavals as Princess Margaret's switch from the minis to the midis. Laver's reassuring word: "Although the midis are in the shop windows, the minis are still in the streets."

III

THERE IS ONE artist in France today whose work displays a strength of passion and eroticism equal to that of Baudelaire's poems, and who likewise achieves his effects by an extremely delicate lightness and sureness of touch that are the antithesis of vulgarity. He is Pierre-Yves Trémois, who has provided ten double-page etchings to illustrate our edition.

In the creations of Trémois, as in the poems of Baudelaire, the animal kingdom

[3]

and the human kingdom meet and are reconciled. Lovers, globes, birds, flowers exist together in a striking harmony which is only possible in the world created by art. As an added grace, each etching includes, in the artist's handwriting, a few lines from the poem it illustrates.

Pierre-Yves Trémois was born in Paris just fifty-two years ago. He attended the École des Beaux-Arts there, received his training in engraving at the Atelier Lacourière, and in 1943 was awarded the coveted Grand Prix de Rome for painting, an honor which entitles the painter to continue his studies at the Villa Medici in Rome.

Returning to Paris the following year he devoted himself to engraving and very soon was illustrating works for such important publishers as Gallimard and Flammarion, as well as numerous bibliophiles. Trémois visited Central Africa in 1956 and made a set of large plates graphically illustrating the amorous behavior of animals; it was published with a text by Rostand and the title *Bestiaire d'Amour*.

He was among a group of leading artists—Dali, Buffet, Foujita, and others—commissioned by the publisher Forêt to paint scenes on parchment for a one-and-only copy of the Apocalypse. Trémois has also engraved a number of original *estampes* to be published in restricted editions. In 1960 he became an Officer of the Legion of Honor (Arts and Letters section).

A visitor to the artist will find his apartment-studio in the fashionable Avenue Marceau. There, after passing through wooden doors from the street to a courtyard and through iron doors to an iron lift which gives a slow and scary ride up three flights, he will be received by his host with wit and courtesy and probably a bottle of champagne. With his stiff grey hair, black eyebrows, and sparkling black eyes, Trémois makes a striking appearance, and his ebullience matches that of his wine.

IV

DESIGNER Charles Skaggs, whose work for The Heritage Club began with *A Connecticut Yankee* in 1946, recently moved from New Jersey to Leitchfield, Kentucky, where he hopes to pursue his freelance career in ecologically undisturbed country. He describes his move as "the return of the native," because it was from Kentucky that he set out thirty-seven years ago to try his luck in the world of graphic arts—first in Chicago, then in New York, where he justifiably acquired a reputation for meticulous and imaginative design.

Of *The Flowers of Evil* he writes:

"I tried for something lean, elegant, yet unfancy and faintly Gallic. The illustrations are so viscerally expressive and linear in style as to rule out any typographic caprice or decoration. Any book of poetry, with all its randomness of pattern, will present problems and surprises. Most designers have found it expedient to yield rather than wield in designing for verse, which seems to require more humility than other literary forms. And in this edition—absolute abasement!"

The result of all Skaggs's typographic care and craftsmanship is this unusually tall and narrow volume, its text set in the 14-point size of Bembo and embellished on the title page with the designer's sparkling calligraphic and roman lettering.

The cream-toned wove paper was made specially for this edition at the Mohawk mills in Cohoes, New York. Credit for the printing of the text and the reproduction of the etchings goes to the Rae Publishing Company of Cedar Grove, New Jersey.

The exterior setting for our poetic jewels was planned to harmonize with the exotic and purple mood of Baudelaire's poems: the gold, blue, and black swirls of the imported French marbled paper on the sides; the rich plum coloring of the linen spine; the label stamping of pure gold leaf on its midnight-dark background. The binding was performed by Tapley-Rutter, under the eye of master jeweler William F. Fortney.

[4]

The whole world to her overflowing dug.
Man elegant, robust and strong, then could
Be proud of the pure beauties he subdued
For they were clean fruit, innocent of blight
Whose succulent firm flesh was good to bite!

The Poet now, if he should hope to meet
This native grandeur in some shady street
Where men and women show themselves undressed
Will feel a cold thrill agitate his breast
In front of that dark, terrible display.
O weeping monsters! cover up from day
Those obscene torsoes, that grotesque disguise,
Those twisted, lean, flabby, pot-bellied bodies,
Which Fashion with inexorable hands
Serenely clamped into brass swaddling-bands!
Alas! You women, whose debauched life aids
That mordant wax-pale canker, and you, maids
To whom your mothers' pestilence will pass
And hideous fecundity, alas!

Though in our decadence we have achieved
Beauty of which no forerunners conceived
In faces wasted with the heart's foul growth
And the new, languid loveliness of sloth
These late imaginations of our muse
Can yet not make a sick old race refuse
To render its deep homage up to youth –
To divine youth's sweet features, simple truth,
To limpid eyes transparent as the spring,
And the glad radiance of everything,
Instinctive as the blue sky, birds and flowers,
Its songs, its perfumes and its soft, warm hours.

[A. GRAHAM REYNOLDS]

VI

The Beacons

Rubens, oblivious garden of indolence,
Pillow of cool flesh where no man dreams of love,
Where life flows forth in troubled opulence,
As airs in heaven and seas in ocean move.

Leonard da Vinci, sombre and fathomless glass,
Where lovely angels with calm lips that smile,
Heavy with mystery, in the shadow pass,
Among the ice and pines that guard some isle.

Rembrandt, sad hospital that a murmuring fills,
Where one tall crucifix hangs on the walls,
Where every tear-drowned prayer some woe distils,
And one cold, wintry ray obliquely falls.

Strong Michelangelo, a vague far place
Where mingle Christs with pagan Hercules;
Thin phantoms of the great through twilight pace,
And tear their shroud with clenched hands void of ease.

The fighter's anger, the faun's impudence,
Thou makest of all these a lovely thing;
Proud heart, sick body, mind's magnificence:
Puget, the convict's melancholy king.

Watteau, the carnival of illustrious hearts,
Fluttering like moths upon the wings of chance;
Bright lustres light the silk that flames and darts,
And pour down folly on the whirling dance.

Goya, a nightmare full of things unknown;
The fetus witches broil on Sabbath night;
Old women at the mirror; children lone
Who tempt old demons with their limbs' delight.

Fruits purs de tout outrage
et vierges de gerçures,

Dont la chair lisse et ferme
appelait les morsures !
...

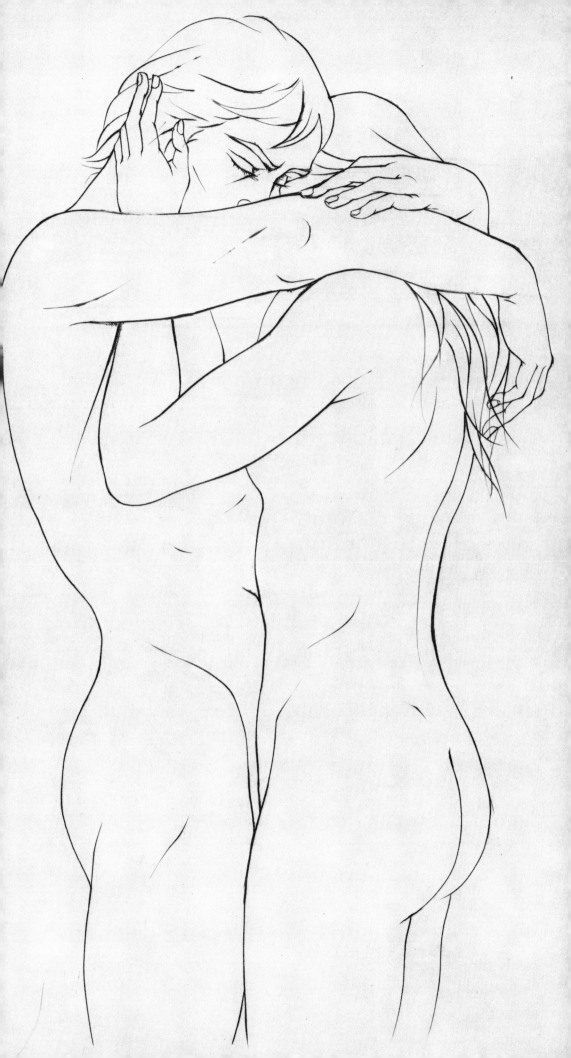

Delacroix, lake of blood ill angels haunt,
Where ever-green, o'ershadowing woods arise;
Under the surly heaven strange fanfares chaunt
And pass, like one of Weber's strangled sighs.

And malediction, blasphemy and groan,
Ecstasies, cries, Te Deums, and tears of brine,
Are echoes through a thousand labyrinths flown;
For mortal hearts an opiate divine;

A shout cried by a thousand sentinels,
An order from a thousand bugles tossed,
A beacon o'er a thousand citadels,
A call to huntsmen in deep woodlands lost.

It is the mightiest witness that could rise
To prove our dignity, O Lord, to Thee;
This sob that rolls from age to age, and dies
Upon the verge of Thy Eternity!

[JAMES HUNEKER]

VII

The Sick Muse

Poor Muse, alas, what ails thee, then, to-day?
Thy hollow eyes with midnight visions burn,
Upon thy brow in alternation play
Madness and Horror, cold and taciturn.

Have the green lemure and the goblin red,
Poured on thee love and terror from their urn?
Or with despotic hand the nightmare dread
Deep plunged thee in some fabulous Minturne?

Would that thy breast where so deep thoughts arise,
Breathed forth a healthful perfume with thy sighs;
Would that thy Christian blood ran wave by wave

In rhythmic sounds the antique numbers gave,
When Phoebus shared his alternating reign
With mighty Pan, lord of the ripening grain.

[JAMES HUNEKER]

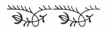

VIII

The Venal Muse

Muse of my heart, lover of palaces,
When January comes with wind and sleet,
During the snowy eve's long wearinesses,
Will there be fire to warm thy violet feet?

Wilt thou reanimate thy marble shoulders
In the moon-beams that through the window fly?
Or when thy purse dries up, thy palace moulders,
Reap the far star-gold of the vaulted sky?

For thou, to keep thy body to thy soul,
Must swing a censer, wear a holy stole,
And chaunt Te Deums with unbelief between.

Or, like a starving mountebank, expose
Thy beauty and thy tear-drowned smile to those
Who wait thy jests to drive away their spleen.

[JAMES HUNEKER]

IX

The Bad Monk

On the great walls of ancient cloisters hung
To warm the inmost heart of piety,
Paintings of holy truth by Scripture sung
Tempered the chill of their austerity.

Illustrious friars, to-day on no one's tongue,
In times when Christ's seed knew prosperity,
Choosing for field the graves they walked among,
Glorified Death in all simplicity.

I, sorry hermit, have my soul for tomb,
Since time began, my walking-place, my room;
Nothing adorns this cloister's odious white.

O idle-fingered monk! when shall I learn
My misery's living spectacle to turn
Into my handiwork, my eyes' delight?

[LORD DERWENT]

X

The Enemy

Naught but a long blind tempest was my youth,
Sun-shot at times; the thunder and the rain
Have worked their havoc with so little ruth
That in my garden few red fruits remain.

Now have I reached the autumn of my thought,
And shovel and pick must use some soil to save
From out the ruins that the rain hath wrought
Where all around great pits gape like the grave.

Who knows if these last flowers of my dreams
Shall find beneath this naked strand that streams
The mystic substance which their strength imparts?

O misery! misery! Time eats our lives,
And that dark Enemy who gnaws our hearts
Grows by the blood he sucks from us, and thrives.

[SIR JOHN SQUIRE]

XI

Unlucky

To lift a load so desperate
Would need your courage, Sisyphus!
Though keen the soul that burns in us,
Yet Art is long, and Time grows late.

Far from illustrious burials,
Towards a graveyard no one knows,
My heart moves, beating as it goes
The muffled drums of funerals.

How many jewels, lost in sleep,
Oblivion and darkness keep
Withdrawn from picks and soundings rude!

And many a flower sighs its scent
Softer than intimacies, pent
In the profoundest solitude.

[LORD DERWENT]

XII

My Former Life

Under vast colonnades that took the noon's
Sea-mirrored fire, I dwelt. In eve's dim light
The pillars showed majestic and upright
Like basalt caves wherein the wroth sea swoons;
The surge that mocked the sun's face and the moon's,
Merged as in solemn and most mystic rite
The hues of sunset waning on my sight
With mighty concord of immortal tunes.

I drank voluptuous calm amid the sheen
Of sea and sky and mirrored light serene;
Where naked slaves with bodies steeped in balms,
Eager to soothe the sorrow undivined
Whereof I grew most weary, fanned the wind
Athwart my brow with wafture of green palms.

[WILFRID THORLEY]

XIII

Gypsies Travelling

The tribe prophetic with the eyes of fire
Went forth last night; their little ones at rest
Each on his mother's back, with his desire
Set on the ready treasure of her breast.

Laden with shining arms the men-folk tread
By the long wagons where their goods lie hidden;
They watch the heaven with eyes grown wearièd
Of hopeless dreams that come to them unbidden.

The grasshopper, from out his sandy screen,
Watching them pass redoubles his shrill song;
Dian, who loves them, makes the grass more green,

And makes the rock run water for this throng
Of ever-wandering ones whose calm eyes see
Familiar realms of darkness yet to be.

[JAMES HUNEKER]

XIV

Man and the Sea

Unto thy roving spirit must the ocean
Be ever dear, O man that dost dislimn
In her vast surges' never-ending motion,
Thy soul unfathomed, and thy bitter whim.

Her bosom is thy joy when thou art cleaving
Its billows; then thine eyes, thine arms are fain,
And thy heart hearing its wild plaint upheaving
Forgets awhile the sound of its own pain.

Both in remote and shadowy ways abiding:
Man, who hath plumbed the deeps of thy dark soul?
O jealous sea, who knows what thou art hiding
Far from our gaze on some unfathomed shoal?

Yet through uncounted time have ye been waging
An unrelenting battle, life for life,
O brothers in dire hatred unassuaging,
In lust of slaughter and eternal strife!

[WILFRID THORLEY]

XV

Don Juan in Hell

The night Don Juan came to pay his fees
To Charon, by the caverned water's shore,
A beggar, proud-eyed as Antisthenes,
Stretched out his knotted fingers on the oar.

Mournful, with drooping breasts and robes unsewn
The shapes of women swayed in ebon skies,
Trailing behind him with a restless moan
Like cattle herded for a sacrifice.

Here, grinning for his wage, stood Sganarelle,
And here Don Luis pointed, bent and dim,
To show the dead who lined the holes of Hell,
This was that impious son who mocked at him.

The hollow-eyed, the chaste Elvira came,
Trembling and veiled, to view her traitor spouse.
Was it one last bright smile she thought to claim,
Such as made sweet the morning of his vows?

A great stone man rose like a tower on board,
Stood at the helm and cleft the flood profound:
But the calm hero, leaning on his sword,
Gazed back, and would not offer one look round.

[JAMES ELROY FLECKER]

XVI

To Théodore de Banville, 1842

So proud your port, your arm so powerful,
With such a grip you grip the goddess' hair,
That one might take you, from your casual air,
For a young ruffian flinging down his trull.

Your clear eye flashing with precocity,
You have displayed yourself proud architect
Of fabrics so audaciously correct
That we may guess what your ripe prime will be.

Poet, our blood ebbs out through every pore;
Is it, perchance, the robe the Centaur bore,
Which made a sullen streamlet of each vein,

Was three times dipped within the venom fell
Of those old reptiles fierce and terrible
Whom, in his cradle, Hercules had slain?

[SIR JOHN SQUIRE]

XVII

The Chastisement of Pride

In those old times wherein Theology
Flourished with greater sap and energy,
A celebrated doctor – so they say –
Having stirred many careless hearts one day
Down to their dullest depths, and having shown
Strange pathways leading to the heavenly throne –
Tracks he himself had never journeyed on

(Whereby maybe pure spirits alone had gone) –
Frenzied and swollen by a devilish pride,
Like to a man who has climbed too high, outcried:
'Ah, little Jesus, I have lifted thee!
But had I willed to assault thy dignity,
Thy shame had matched thy present fame, and lo!
Thou wouldst be but a wretched embryo!'

Straightway his reason left him; that keen mind,
Sunbright before, was darkened and made blind;
All chaos whirled within that intellect
Erewhile a shrine with all fair gems bedeckt,
Beneath whose roof such pomp had shone so bright;
He was possessed by silence and thick night
As is a cellar when its key is lost . . . .

Thenceforth he was a brute beast; when he crossed
The fields at times, not seeing any thing,
Knowing not if 'twere winter or green spring,
Useless, repulsive, vile, he made a mock
For infants, a mere children's laughing-stock.

[SIR JOHN SQUIRE]

XVIII

Beauty

Fair am I, mortals, as a stone-carved dream,
And all men wound themselves against my breast,
The poet's last desire, the loveliest.
Voiceless, eternal as the world I seem.
In the blue air, strange sphinx, I brood supreme
With heart of snow whiter than swan's white crest,
No movement mars the plastic line – I rest
With lips untaught to laugh or eyes to stream.

Singers who see, in trancèd interludes,
My splendour set with all superb design,
Consume their days, in toilful ecstasy.
To these revealed, the starry amplitudes
Of my great eyes which make all things divine
Are crystal mirrors of eternity.

[LORD ALFRED DOUGLAS]

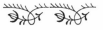

XIX

The Ideal

Not all the beauties in old prints vignetted,
The worthless products of an outworn age,
With slippered feet and fingers castanetted,
The thirst of hearts like this heart can assuage.

To Gavarni, the poet of chloroses,
I leave his troupes of beauties sick and wan;
I cannot find among these pale, pale roses,
The red ideal mine eyes would gaze upon.

Lady Macbeth, the lovely star of crime,
The Greek poet's dream born in a northern clime –
Ah, she could quench my dark heart's deep desiring;

Or Michelangelo's dark daughter Night,
In a strange posture dreamily admiring
Her beauty fashioned for a giant's delight!

[JAMES HUNEKER]

XX

The Giantess

When Nature in her lavish lustiness
Bred day by day new, strange monstrosities,
Would I had lived with a young giantess
Like a warm cat who at a queen's feet lies.

'Twere sweet to watch her soul and body blossom
While she disported her in terrible wise;
To guess if a fierce flame burnt in her bosom
By the wet mists that swam within her eyes.

Ah! freely o'er her mighty limbs to run,
To crawl upon the bend of her vast knees,
And when in summer, tired of the pestilent sun,
Across the plain she stretches calm and still,
Within her breasts' cool shade to sleep at ease
Like some small hamlet sheltered by a hill.

[SIR JOHN SQUIRE]

XXI

The Mask

(AN ALLEGORICAL STATUE IN THE STYLE OF THE RENAISSANCE)

Observe the Florentine grand style, and trace
How in this body's sinuous soft curves
Twin goddesses are present, Force and Grace;
Truly she is miraculous, deserves
In her delicious strength and suppleness
To be enthroned on some most sumptuous bed
And charm a king's or pontiff's idleness.

Observe again where self-conceit is led
To steal enjoyment from this tempting smile;
This languid, sinister and mocking air;
This coy regard, concealed beneath a veil,
In which victorious lineaments declare
'I am called Pleasure, and am crowned by Love.'
What thrilling charm informs her majesty
This moving gentleness goes far to prove.
Let us go near and walk around her beauty.

Oh! blasphemy of art! oh! fatal shock!
The divine body, which appeared to ask
Us to our pleasure, has two heads that mock!

No! these exquisite features are a mask,
Mere debased ornament with fine grimace;
Behind, atrociously contorted, is
The veritable head, the sincere face
Turned to the shadow of this face which lies.
Poor perfect beauty, a grand river breaks
As your tears fall into my anxious soul,
I am drunk with your lie, my spirit slakes
Its torture in the stream your eyes unroll.

Why is she weeping? In her lovely pride
She could have conquered the whole race of man;
What unknown evil harrows her lithe side?

She weeps, mad girl, because her life began;
Because she lives. One thing she does deplore
So much that she kneels trembling in the dust –
That she must live to-morrow, evermore,
To-morrow and to-morrow – as we must!

[A. GRAHAM REYNOLDS]

XXII

Hymn to Beauty

Comest thou from high heaven or from the abyss,
O Beauty? For thy look, hellish, divine,
Is fraught with mingled misery and bliss
(Wherefore thy soul is as the soul of wine).

Within thine eye red dawn and sunset burn;
Odours thou spread'st as stormy evenings;
Thy kisses are a draught, thy mouth an urn
To make men quail and babes do mighty things.

From the dark gulf, or from the immortal stars?
The charmèd Demon follows like a hound;
Thou rul'st with hand that careless makes or mars,
Nor to our prayers vouchsafest any sound.

Thou walkest over dead men, mocking them,
Beauty! and horror decks the throat of thee,
And glittering murder, thy most precious gem,
On thy proud belly dances amorously.

Toward thee, flame, the dazzled insect flies,
Shrivels and cries, 'Blest conqueror of gloom!'
Upon his fair one's breast the lover lies,
As 'twere a dying man who hugs his tomb.

Naïve, terrible form! what boots it sky or pit,
O Beauty! if thine eye, smile, foot, alone
Can open me the gate of an infinite
My soul's athirst for, and has never known?

What boots it, seraph or siren, from God's height
Or Satan's hell, O queen! if thou dost come
Soft-eyed, to make, with rhythm, scent, and light,
The world less dull and time less burdensome?

[SIR JOHN SQUIRE]

XXIII

Exotic Perfume

In autumn twilight, when with fast closed eyes
I breathe the fragrance of thy fervent breast,
About me spreads a reach of changeless skies,
And sunlit dazzling shores in happy rest.
A drowsy isle, the dainty forcing place
Of luscious fruits, and strange gigantic trees,
The sultry dwelling of a slender race
Whose girls are frank and lightsome as the breeze.

Led thus by dreams towards these sunset climes,
I gaze upon a crowded port, a throng
Of masts and sails, an open windswept sea,
Whilst from the land the perfume of the limes
Makes sweet the air, and comes across to me
Blent with the chorus of a sailor's song.

[EUGENE MASON]

XXIV

The Hair

O billows flowing o'er the shoulders bare!
O curls! O perfume sweet beyond belief!
Here in this bower to people the night air
With all the memories sleeping in this hair
I long to shake it like a handkerchief!

Fierce Afric and the languorous Orient,
All a vast world, distant, nay, almost dead,
Within this aromatic wood is pent;
My soul beloved floats upon thy scent
As other souls have music for a bed.

De Satan ou

Qu'importe, si tu rends,
    — Fée aux yeux

Rhythme, parfum, lueur,

        Ô mon unique reine

    L'univers moins hideux

            et les instants

Dieu, qu'importe ?
Ange ou Sirêne,

lours,

ores lourds ?

I will go out where full-veined man and tree
Swoon daylong in the sultry summer's heat –
Strong tresses be the barque which carries me:
Thou holdest a bright dream, O ebon sea,
Of sails, flames, rowers, on a splendid fleet;

A harbour where through every sense are rolled
Vast sweeping waves of perfume, sound, and hue,
Where vessels gliding over moire and gold
Stretch up great arms to heaven to enfold
The glory of the everlasting blue.

There waits for me delicious drunkenness
In this dark sea which holds those other seas;
My spirit in the gentle main's caress
Shall know once more the old rich idleness,
Infinite rockings of embalmèd ease.

Ah! dark-blue, streaming banner of the night,
You bring me back those azure skies afar,
Plunged in your silken folds my soul takes flight
And drinks once more with measureless delight
The scent of cocoa-oil and musk and tar.

For ever I will scatter in each strand,
That thou may'st never turn deaf ears to me,
Rubies, pearls, sapphires with a lavish hand . . . .
Thou art the well-spring in a desert land
Wherefrom I quaff deep draughts of memory.

[SIR JOHN SQUIRE]

XXV

Je t'adore...

You, whom I worship as night's firmament,
Urn of my sorrow, beautiful and silent,
I love you more, because you turn from me
Adorning night, but, with large irony
Rather increase the absolute blue space
Which alienates the sky from my embrace.

I leap to your attack, climb in assault
Like corpseworms feeding nimbly in the vault,
And cherish you, relentless, cruel beast
Till that last coldness which delights me best.

[A. GRAHAM REYNOLDS]

XXVI

Tu mettrais l'univers...

You'd take the entire universe to bed with you,
I think, just out of boredom, you lecherous, idle shrew!
You need, to keep your teeth sound, exercise your jaws,
Daily, for dinner, some new heart between your paws!
Your eyes, all lighted up like shops, like public fairs,
How insolent they are! – as if their power were theirs
Indeed! – this borrowed power, this Beauty, you direct
And use, whose law, however, you do not suspect.

Unwholesome instrument for health, O deaf machine
And blind, fecund in tortures! – how is it you have
　　not seen,

You drinker of the world's blood, your mirrored loveliness
Blench and recoil? how is it you feel no shame? confess:
Has never, then, this evil's very magnitude
Caused you to stagger? – you, who think yourself
   so shrewd
In evil? – seeing how Nature, patient and abstruse –
O Woman, Queen of Sins, Vile Animal, – has made use
Of you, to mould a genius? – employed you all this time?

O muddy grandeur! – ignominy ironic and sublime!

[EDNA ST. VINCENT MILLAY]

XXVII

Sed non satiata

Bizarre Deity, dark as infernal nights,
Whose perfume mixes with musk Arabian,
Work of some Obi, Faustus, that learned man,
Sorceress with ebony thighs, child of midnights,
I prefer to all things, opium and the nights,
Thy mouth's elixir, strange as a Pavane;
When toward thee my desires in caravan
Pass, thine eyes assuage mine appetites.
By those black eyes, vent-holes of thy soul's shame,
O pitiless Demon, pour on me less flame;
I am not the Styx to embrace thee nine times, nay,
Alas! I cannot, Megaera of the Sorrows nine,
To break thy courage and to set thee at bay
In the hell of thy bed become thy Proserpine!

[ARTHUR SYMONS]

XXVIII

Avec ses vêtements...

In undulant robes with nacreous sheen impearled
She walks as in some stately saraband;
Or like lithe snakes by sacred charmers curled
In cadence wreathing on the slender wand.

Calm as blue wastes of sky and desert sand
That watch unmoved the sorrows of this world;
With slow regardless sweep as on the strand
The long swell of the woven sea-waves swirled.

Her polished orbs are like a mystic gem,
And, while this strange and symbolled being links
The inviolate angel and the antique sphinx,

Insphered in gold, steel, light and diadem
The splendour of a lifeless star endows
With clear cold majesty the barren spouse.

[WILLIAM JOHN ROBERTSON]

XXIX

The Dancing Snake

I love to watch your indolent
Lovely body move.
Gleams upon your iridescent
Dark skin I love.

Your hair is like a mighty sea,
Wherein men may drown;
Deep, scented, wild immensity
With waves blue and brown!

Like to a ship that spreads its wings
When dawn winds rise,
My soul begins its wanderings
Towards distant skies.

Your dreaming eyes, upon me bent,
Love nor hate reveal,
Cold jewels they, in which are blent
Gleams of gold and steel.

When your languid flanks awake,
And your limbs unbend,
You're like a writhing, dancing snake
On a cudgel's end.

You bear the weight of idle hours,
As heavy as lead,
As lightly as a wreath of flowers
On a baby's head.

Your body's like a graceful ship,
As you bend to me,
That rides the waves, and seems to dip
Its prow in the sea.

Like to a stream that knows no drouth,
Glaciers beneath,
When mounts the moisture of your mouth
Up to your white teeth,

I seem to drink Bohemian wine,
In my wild desire.
What pain and triumph then are mine!
My heart's all fire.

[JAMES LAVER]

XXX

A Carrion

Rememberest thou, my sweet, that summer's day,
How in the sun outspread
At a path's bend a filthy carcase lay
Upon a pebbly bed?

Like a lewd woman, with its legs in air,
Burned, oozed the poisonous mass;
Its gaping belly, calm and debonair,
Was full of noisome gas.

And steadily upon this rottenness,
As though to cook it brown
And render Nature hundredfold excess,
The sun shone down.

The blue sky thought the carrion marvellous,
A flower most fair to see;
And as we gazed it almost poisoned us –
It stank so horribly.

The flies buzzed on this putrid belly, whence
Black hosts of maggots came,
Which streamed in thick and shining rivers thence
Along that ragged frame.

Pulsating like a wave, spirting about
Bright jets, it seemed to live;
As though it were by some vague wind blown out,
Some breath procreative.

And all this life was strangely musical
Like wind or bubbling spring,
Or corn which moves with rhythmic rise and fall
In time of winnowing.

The lines became indefinite and faint
As a thin dream that dies,
A half-forgotten scene the hand can paint
Only from memories . . .

Behind the rocks there lurked a hungry hound
With melancholy eye,
Longing to nose the morsel he had found
And gnaw it greedily.

Yet thou shalt be as vile a carrion
As this infection dire,
O bright star of my eyes, my nature's sun,
My angel, my desire!

Yea, such, O queen of the graces, shalt thou be
After the last soft breath,
Beneath the grass and the lush greenery
A-mouldering in death!

When thy sweet flesh the worms devour with kisses,
Tell them, O beauty mine,
Of rotting loves I keep the bodily blisses
And essence all-divine!

[SIR JOHN SQUIRE]

XXXI

De Profundis Clamavi

O my sole love, I pray thee pity me
From out this dark gulf where my poor heart lies
A barren world hemmed in by leaden skies
Where horror flies at night, and blasphemy.

For half the year the sickly sun is seen,
The other half thick night lies on the land,
A country bleaker than the polar strand;
No beasts, no brooks, nor any shred of green.

There never was a horror which surpassed
This icy sun's cold cruelty, and this vast
Night like primeval Chaos; would I were

Like the dumb brutes, who in a secret lair
Lie wrapt in stupid slumber for a space . . .
The time creeps at so burdensome a pace.

[SIR JOHN SQUIRE]

XXXII

The Vampire

Thou who abruptly as a knife
Didst come into my heart; thou who,
A demon horde into my life,
Didst enter, wildly dancing, through

The doorways of my sense unlatched
To make my spirit thy domain –
Harlot to whom I am attached
As convicts to the ball and chain,

As gamblers to the wheel's bright spell,
As drunkards to their raging thirst,
As corpses to their worms – accurst
Be thou! Oh, be thou damned to hell!

I have entreated the swift sword
To strike, that I at once be freed;
The poisoned phial I have implored
To plot with me a ruthless deed.

Alas! the phial and the blade
Do cry aloud and laugh at me:
'Thou art not worthy of our aid;
Thou art not worthy to be free.

'Though one of us should be the tool
To save thee from thy wretched fate,
Thy kisses would resuscitate
The body of thy vampire, fool!'

[GEORGE DILLON]

XXXIII

Une nuit que j'étais près . . .

A hideous Jewess lay with me for hire
One night: two corpses side by side we seemed
And stretched by that polluted thing I dreamed
Of the sad beauty of my vain desire.

I thought upon her brow clad round with fire
And matchless strength, her native majesty,
Her perfumed helm of hair whose memory
Makes me toward Love's heights to reaspire.

For fervently I would have rained, my Sweet,
Fond kisses over all thy form divine
Even from thy black tresses to thy feet,

If some soft evening, with a single tear,
O cruel queen, thou couldst have dimmed the clear
Cold splendour of those icy eyes of thine.

[SIR JOHN SQUIRE]

XXXIV

Posthumous Remorse

When thou shalt sleep, O beauty ebon-hued!
Beneath a marble blacker than thy thighs,
And thou shalt have to honour thy dead eyes
Only a clammy cavern; when the lewd
Head-stone upon thy slumber shall intrude
Bruising thy flank, thy bosom; when thy sighs
Shall ebb for ever, and thy feet likewise
Fail on the path of peril once pursued,

The grave that to my endless dream gives heed,
(For with the poet doth the grave conspire),
As night by night the unsleeping hours retire,
Shall say, 'Why, foolish harlot! hadst thou need
To flout dead grief?' Then on thy flesh like fire
The worm remorse for evermore shall feed.

[WILFRID THORLEY]

XXXV

The Cat

Come, lovely cat, to this adoring breast;
Over thy daggers silken scabbards draw;
Into thy beauty let me plunge to rest,
Unmindful of thy swift and cruel claw,

The while my fingers leisurely caress
Thy head and vaulted back's elastic arch,
And through each tip mysterious pleasures press
And crackle on their swift dynamic march.

I see revived in thee, felinely cast
A woman with thine eyes, satanic beast,
Profound and cold as scythes to mow me down.

And from her feet up to her throat are massed
Strange aromas; a perfume from the East
Swims round her body, sinuous and brown.

[COUNTEE CULLEN]

XXXVI

Duellum

Two warriors have charg'd, have met; thrusts' fire
Has splash'd the air with spurt of light and gore.
This play, this clash of steel the mere uproar
As young blood mewls at stirring of desire.

The glaives are shatter'd! like our shatter'd youth,
My dear! But sword and dirk which cheat their trust
Are soon aveng'd by steelèd nail and tooth,
Mature heart's frenzy festering with lust!

Down into the gulf, that pard and tiger lair,
Our heroes grimly intergripp'd have roll'd,
Their skin shall prink the dry bones of the thorn.

– This abyss, 'tis Hell, throng'd with our friends. O there,
Inhuman Amazon, let us reel and hold
Eterniz'd so our fire of hate and scorn!

[ARTHUR ELLIS]

XXXVII

The Balcony

Mother of Memories! O mistress-queen!
Oh! all my joy and all my duty thou!
The beauty of caresses that have been,
The evenings and the hearth remember now,
Mother of Memories! O mistress-queen!

The evenings burning with the glowing fire,
And on the balcony, the rose-stained nights!
How sweet, how kind you were, my soul's desire.
We said things wonderful as chrysolites,
When evening burned beside the glowing fire.

How fair the Sun is in the evening!
How strong the soul, how high the heaven's high tower!
O first and last of every worshipped thing,
Your odorous heart's-blood filled me like a flower.
How fair the sun is in the evening!

The night grew deep between us like a pall,
And in the dark I guessed your shining eyes,
And drank your breath, O sweet, O honey-gall!
Your little feet slept on me sister-wise.
The night grew deep between us like a pall.

I can call back the days desirable,
And live all bliss again between your knees,
For where else can I find that magic spell
Save in your heart and in your Mysteries?
I can call back the days desirable.

These vows, these scents, these kisses infinite,
Will they like young suns climbing up the skies
Rise up from some unfathomable pit,
Washed in the sea from all impurities?
O vows, O scents, O kisses infinite!

[LORD ALFRED DOUGLAS]

XXXVIII

The Possessed One

The sun is enveloped in crape! like it,
O Moon of my Life! wrap thyself up in shade;
At will, smoke or slumber, be silent, be staid,
And dive deep down in Dispassion's dark pit.

I cherish thee thus! But if 'tis thy mood,
Like a star that from out its penumbra appears,
To float in the regions where madness careers,
Fair dagger! burst forth from thy sheath! 'tis good.

Yea, light up thine eyes at the Fire of Renown!
Or kindle desire by the looks of some clown!
Thine All is my joy, whether dull or aflame!

Just be what thou wilt, black night, dawn divine,
There is not a nerve in my trembling frame
But cries, 'I adore thee, Beelzebub mine!'

[CYRIL SCOTT]

XXXIX

A Phantom

I. IN THE SHADOWS

Down in the fathomless despair
Where Destiny has locked me in,
Where light nor joy descends, and where
– Sole lodger of Night's dreary inn,

Like artists blind God sets apart
In mockery, I paint the murk;
Where, ghoulish scullion, I work
Boiling and munching all my heart,

Glitters anon, and grows apace
A phantom languorous and bright,
A dream of Oriental grace,

When it attains its utmost height,
I know at last the lovely thing:
'Tis She! girl dark yet glimmering.

II. THE PERFUME

Hast thou inhaled – O reader, say! –
With zest and lazy greed, the old
Incense that chapel arches hold
Or the stale musk of a sachet?

O magic spell, O ecstasy!
– To make the present yield the past! –
'Tis thus on a beloved breast
Love culls the flowers of memory.

The tresses long about her face
– A living censer, left the place
With strange wild odours all astir,

And in her velvet, muslin, lace,
Candid and girlish, over her
Hovered a perfume faint of fur.

III. THE PICTURE FRAME

A fine frame to a picture brings
– Though from a brush illustrious –
A charm strange and mysterious,
Secluding it from other things.

Thus jewels, metals, gold, became
Adapted to her beauty bright;
Nothing obscured its perfect light,
All things about her seemed a frame.

Full oft one might have said she found
Her garments loved her, for she drowned
In amorous satins, lacy nets,

Her body, bare and shivering,
And, slow or swift, her posturing
Was graceful as a marmoset's.

IV. THE PORTRAIT

Death and Disease make ashes of
The flames that wrapped our youth around.
Of her soft eyes, ablaze with love,
Her mouth, wherein my heart was drowned,

Of her long kisses' magic spell,
Her passion, sharp as Phoebus' dart,
What have I now? O woeful heart!
Naught but a faded old pastel.

Dying, like me, in solitude,
Paling each day in every part
'Neath Time's untiring pinions rude . . .

Dark murderer of Life and Art,
Never shalt thou in me destroy
Her who was once my pride and joy!

[LEWIS PIAGET SHANKS]

XL

Je te donne ces vers . . .

These lines to thee, that if my name should come
To Time's far harbours, on a favouring main,
And driven by the tempest, find a home,
Some evening, in a poet's dreaming brain,

That thoughts of thee, like legends vague and vain,
May tire my reader as a mighty drum,
And linked in mystic union, may become
A symbol married to this lofty strain;

Accursèd one, to whom, from the deep skies
To the Abyss, naught, save my heart, replies;
– O thou that like a ghost impalpable

Tramplest upon, serenely as a bonze,
The stupid mortals who denied thy spell,
Cold statue, jet-eyed angel cast in bronze!

[LEWIS PIAGET SHANKS]

XLI

Semper Eadem

Dost ask: 'Whence cometh all thy sadness strange,
A mounting tide against a grey sea-wall?'
When hearts have culled their grapes in Love's exchange,
To live is hateful. Secret known to all,

A common sorrow, free from mysteries,
'Tis like thy joy a glaring thing enow.
So, Lady Curious, thy searching cease!
And though thy voice is sweet, be silent now!

Be silent, simple heart, forever gay
With girlish laughter! More than Life, to-day,
Death binds our hearts in tenuous webs of doom.

Let me be drunken with the wine of *lies,*
Leave me to delve for dreams within thine eyes,
And slumber long beneath thine eyebrows' gloom!

[LEWIS PIAGET SHANKS]

XLII

Tout Entière

This morning in my attic high
The Demon came to visit me,
And seeking faults in my reply,
He said: 'I would inquire of thee,

'Of all the beauties which compose
Her charming body's potent spell,
Of all the objects black and rose
Which make the thing you love so well,

'Which is the sweetest?' O my soul!
Thou didst rejoin: 'How tell of parts,
When all I know is that the whole
Works magic in my heart of hearts?

'Where all is fair, how should I say
What single grace is my delight?
She shines on me like break of day
And she consoles me as the night.

'There flows through all her perfect frame
A harmony too exquisite
That weak analysis should name
The numberless accords of it.

'O mystic metamorphosis!
My separate senses all are blent;
Within her breath soft music is,
And in her voice a subtle scent!'

[SIR JOHN SQUIRE]

XLIII

Que diras-tu ce soir...

Poor soul, what word comes from thy loneliness,
What word, my heart, remembering old mischance,
Unto that utter Beauty that can bless
Anew thy being with her godlike glance?
'Her do we praise with our proud melodies.
There is nought sweeter than her sacred might
Whose flesh is scented as an angel's is,
Whose glance clothes all things in unstainèd light.

'Whether it be in darkness where none bide
Or in the sunlit street by many trod,
Her ghost goes fluttering like a flame in air.
She saith: "I, who am lovely, bid thee guide
Thy heart to follow Beauty everywhere,
I who am Angel, Muse, and Mother of God!" '

[WILFRID THORLEY]

XLIV

The Living Flame

They pass before me, these Eyes full of light,
Eyes made magnetic by some angel wise;
The holy brothers pass before my sight,
And cast their diamond fires in my dim eyes.

They keep me from all sin and error grave,
They set me in the path whence Beauty came;
They are my servants, and I am their slave,
And all my soul obeys the living flame.

Beautiful Eyes that gleam with mystic light
As candles lighted at full noon; the sun
Dims not your flame phantastical and bright.

You sing the dawn; they celebrate life done;
Marching you chaunt my soul's awakening hymn,
Stars that no sun has ever made grow dim!

[JAMES HUNEKER]

XLV

Reversibility

Angel of gaiety, have you tasted grief?
Shame and remorse and sobs and weary spite,
And the vague terrors of the fearful night
That crush the heart up like a crumpled leaf?
Angel of gaiety, have you tasted grief?

Angel of kindness, have you tasted hate?
With hands clenched in the shade and tears of gall,
When Vengeance beats her hellish battle-call,
And makes herself the captain of our fate,
Angel of kindness, have you tasted hate?

Angel of health, did ever you know pain,
Which like an exile trails his tired footfalls
The cold length of the white infirmary walls,
With lips compressed, seeking the sun in vain?
Angel of health, did ever you know pain?

Angel of beauty, do you wrinkles know?
Know you the fear of age, the torment vile
Of reading secret horror in the smile
Of eyes your eyes have loved since long ago?
Angel of beauty, do you wrinkles know?

Angel of happiness, and joy, and light,
Old David would have asked for youth afresh
From the pure touch of your enchanted flesh;
I but implore your prayers to aid my plight,
Angel of happiness, and joy, and light.

[JAMES HUNEKER]

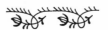

XLVI

The Confession

Once, only once, beloved and gentle lady,
Upon my arm you leaned your arm of snow,
And on my spirit's background, dim and shady,
That memory flashes now.

The hour was late, and like a medal gleaming
The full moon showed her face,
And the night's splendour over Paris streaming
Filled every silent place.

Along the houses, in the doorways hiding,
Cats passed with stealthy tread
And listening ear, or followed, slowly gliding,
Like ghosts of dear ones dead.

Sudden, amid our frank and free relation,
Born of that limpid light,
From you, rich instrument, whose sole vibration
Was radiancy and light—

From you, joyous as bugle-call resounding
Across the woods at morn,
With sharp and faltering accent, strangely sounding,
Escaped one note forlorn.

Like some misshapen infant, dark, neglected,
Its kindred blush to own,
And long have hidden, by no eye detected,
In some dim cave unknown.

Your clashing note cried clear, poor, prisoned spirit,
That nothing in the world is sure or fast,
And that man's selfishness, though decked as merit,
Betrays itself at last.

That hard the lot to be a queen of beauty,
And all is fruitless, like the treadmill toil
Of some paid dancer, fainting at her duty,
Still with her vacant smile.

That if one build on hearts, ill shall befall it,
That all things crack, and love and beauty flee,
Until oblivion flings them in his wallet,
Spoil of eternity.

Oft have I called to mind that night enchanted,
The silence and the languor over all,
And that wild confidence, thus harshly chanted,
At the heart's confessional.

[LOIS SAUNDERS]

XLVII

The Spiritual Dawn

When upon revellers the stained dawn breaks
The fierce ideal comes with it; at that hour,
Stirred by some terrible avenging power,
An angel in the sated brute awakes.

Above the stricken, suffering man there glow
Far azure plains of unimagined bliss
Which draw his dreaming spirit like the abyss.
O pure, beloved Goddess, even so

O'er the smoked wrecks of stupid scenes of shame
Brighter and rosier thy sweet memory
Hovers before my wide eyes hauntingly . . .

The Sun has dimmed and charred the candles' flame,
And thus, my glorious all-conquering one,
Thy shade is peer to the immortal Sun.

[SIR JOHN SQUIRE]

XLVIII

Evening Harmony

Now is the hour when, swinging in the breeze,
Each flower, like a censer, sheds its sweet.
The air is full of scents and melodies,
O languorous waltz! O swoon of dancing feet!

Each flower, like a censer, sheds its sweet,
The violins are like sad souls that cry,
O languorous waltz! O swoon of dancing feet!
A shrine of Death and Beauty is the sky.

The violins are like sad souls that cry,
Poor souls that hate the vast black night of Death;
A shrine of Death and Beauty is the sky.
Drowned in red blood, the Sun gives up his breath.

This soul that hates the vast black night of Death
Takes all the luminous past back tenderly,
Drowned in red blood, the Sun gives up his breath.
Thine image like a monstrance shines in me.

[LORD ALFRED DOUGLAS]

XLIX

The Flask

There are some powerful odours that can pass
Out of the stoppered flagon; even glass
To them is porous. Oft when some old box
Brought from the East is opened and the locks
And hinges creak and cry; or in a press
In some deserted house, where the sharp stress
Of odours old and dusty fills the brain;
An ancient flask is brought to light again,
And forth the ghosts of long-dead odours creep.
There, softly trembling in the shadows, sleep
A thousand thoughts, funereal chrysalides,
Phantoms of old the folding darkness hides,
Who make faint flutterings as their wings unfold,
Rose-washed and azure-tinted, shot with gold.

A memory that brings languor flutters here:
The fainting eyelids droop, and giddy Fear
Thrusts with both hands the soul towards the pit
Where, like a Lazarus from his winding-sheet,
Arises from the gulf of sleep a ghost
Of an old passion, long since loved and lost.
So I, when vanished from man's memory
Deep in some dark and sombre chest I lie,
An empty flagon they have cast aside,
Broken and soiled, the dust upon my pride,
Will be your shroud, beloved pestilence!
The witness of your might and virulence,
Sweet poison mixed by angels; bitter cup
Of life and death my heart has drunken up!

[JAMES HUNEKER]

L

Poison

Wine in a sordid hovel can diffuse
A pomp miraculous,
Evoke long temple-arches fabulous
That red and gold suffuse,
As sunset gilds her porches nebulous.

Opium enlarges space: new skies are born
In its infinity;
Moments grow hours, pleasures cease to be;
Its dreary joys forlorn
Vanquish the soul with sensual tyranny.

Dread poisons, but more dread the poisoned well
Of thy green eyes accurst;
Lakes where I view my trembling soul, reversed . . .
My dreams innumerable
Come to thy bitter gulfs to slake their thirst.

Dread magic, but thy mouth more dread than these:
Its wine and hellebore
Burn, floods of Lethe, in my bosom's core,
Till winds of madness seize
And dash me swooning on Death's barren shore!

[LEWIS PIAGET SHANKS]

LI

Sky Overcast

Thy glance is veiled with shadows vaporous;
Grey, blue or green, thine eyes mysterious
—Cruel or soft in turn with reveries—
Reflect the languor of the pallid skies.

Je vois avec étonnement
Le feu de ses prunelles pâles,

Clairs fanaux, vivantes opales
Qui me contemplent fixement

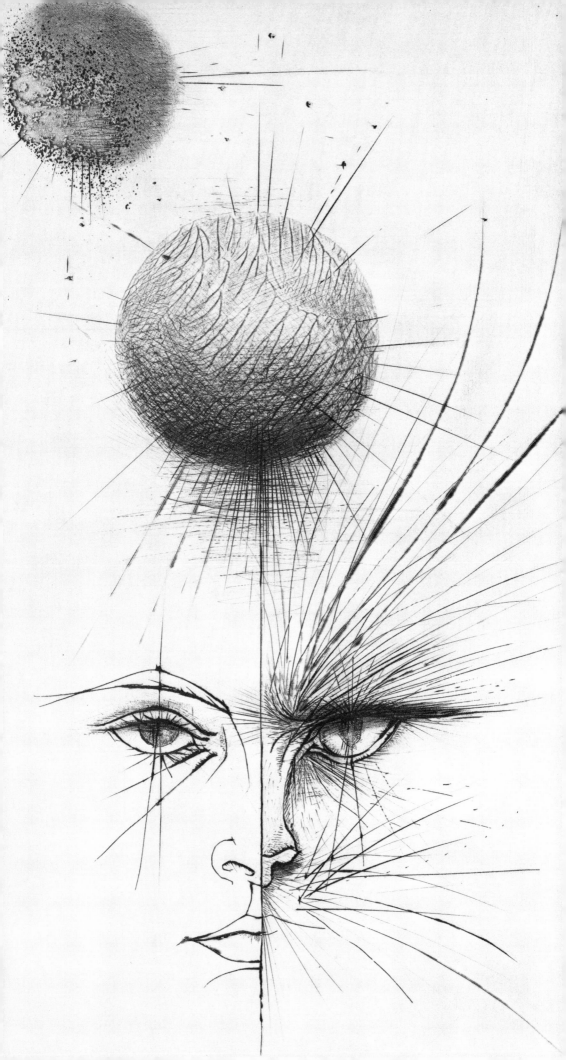

Thou'rt like a soft white morn of silver grey,
Whose magic melts the heart to tears: a day
When by a secret evil racked and torn,
The quivering nerves laugh dormant wits to scorn.

Full oft thou art like fair horizons far
Lit by the suns of days crepuscular . . .
How bright your lustre, dripping woods that lie
Flaming in sunlight from a ruffled sky!

O fateful woman! O entrancing clime!
And shall I also love thy snow, its rime,
And can I wrest from winter's clutch abhorred
New pleasures keen as splintered ice or sword?

[LEWIS PIAGET SHANKS]

LII

The Cat

I

She prowls around my shadowy brain,
As she were mistress of the place,
A furtive beast of charming ways,
Meowing in melodious strain,

Yet so discreetly, softly, her
Angry or peaceful moods resound,
You scarcely hear their song profound,
Her secret, rich, voluptuous purr.

O droning, penetrating cry,
That creeps into my heart perverse,
And drowns it like a rippling verse,
Or love-draught drugged with sorcery!

No tortures that it cannot lull,
No ecstasy but it contains;
No phrase so long but its refrains
Can voice it, wordless, wonderful.

Nay, never master's bow divine,
Rending my heart-strings like a sword,
Rang, vibrant, in so rich a chord,
Such royal harmony as thine,

As thine, mysterious cat, methinks,
Feline seraphic, weird and strange,
Angel of subtlety and change,
Imperial, melodious sphynx!

II

Golden and brown, her tawny fur
Secretes an odour ravishing;
Her spell perfumes the evening,
Although I hardly fondle her.

She is the spirit of the shrine;
Never a deed nor a desire
She does not judge, direct, inspire;
Is she perchance a beast divine?

For when my amorous glances, fain
Of her enchantment, slowly turn
Toward their lode-stone and discern
This prowling creature of my brain,

Startled and marvelling I see
The fire of her pupils pale,
Clear harbour-lights no vapours veil,
Like living opals, holding me.

[LEWIS PIAGET SHANKS]

LIII

The Beautiful Ship

My desire is to respire thy charms that are divine
And all in thee that is more beautiful than wine,
All this desire of mine
Is to paint the child whose fashions are malign.

When thou dost wander thy skirt balances to and fro
In the wind's embraces from the seas that flow,
I see in thee a painted show
Following an ardent rhythm, languid and slow.

On thy large neck, so pure and undefiled,
Thy dear head flaunts itself like dancers, wild,
And I the Exiled
Follow thy subtle footsteps, majestic child!

My desire is to respire thy charms that are divine
And all in thee that is more beautiful than wine,
All this desire of mine
Is to paint the child whose fashions are malign.

Thine ardent breasts advance to meet the air
Triumphant as the silk that hides them and rare
As dancing-girls in vair
That leave thee to the winds that are most fair.

Provoking breasts, with their red points of roses!
Secret to none, as any shy rose that uncloses,
Where perfume with scent dozes
Delirious to the hearts wherein no rest reposes!

When thou dost wander thy skirt balances to and fro
In the wind's embraces from the seas that flow,
I see in thee a painted show
Following an ardent rhythm, languid and slow.

Thy noble legs under their draperies bewitching
Torment obscure desires, set my nerves twitching,
Like two Sorcerers pitching
Black drugs to a snake whose ardent coils are itching.

Thy lovely arms that wave luxuriously
Like unto shining coiling boas furiously
Press one's heart obstinately
And leave me, thy Lover, lonely as the Sea.

On thy large neck, so pure and undefiled,
Thy dear head flaunts itself like dancers, wild,
And I the Exiled
Follow thy subtle footsteps, majestic child!

[ARTHUR SYMONS]

LIV

The Invitation to the Voyage

How sweet, my own,
Could we live alone
Over beyond the sea!
To love and to die
Indolently
In the land that's akin to thee!
Where the suns which rise
In the watery skies
Weave soft spells over my sight,
As thy false eyes do
When they flicker through
Their tears with a dim, strange light.

There all is beauty and symmetry,
Pleasure and calm and luxury.

Years that have gone
Have polished and shone
The things that would fill our room;
The flowers most rare
Which scent the air
In the richly-ceiling'd gloom,
And the mirrors profound,
And the walls around
With Orient splendour hung,
To the soul would speak
Of things she doth seek
In her gentle native tongue.

There all is beauty and symmetry,
Pleasure and calm and luxury.

The canals are deep
Where the strange ships sleep
Far from the land of their birth;
To quench the fire
Of thy least desire
They have come from the ends of the earth.
The sunsets drown
Peaceful town
And meadow, and stagnant stream
In bistre and gold
And the world enfold
In a warm and luminous dream.

There all is beauty and symmetry,
Pleasure and calm and luxury.

[SIR JOHN SQUIRE]

LV

The Irreparable

I

How shall we kill this old, this long Remorse
Which writhes continually
And feeds on us as worms upon a corse,
Maggots upon a tree?
How stifle this implacable Remorse?

What wine, what drug, what philtre known of man
Will drown this ancient foe,
Ruthless and ravenous as a courtesan,
Sure as an ant, and slow?
What wine? What drug? What philtre known of man?

O tell, fair sorceress, tell if thou dost know
This soul distraught with pain
As a dying soldier crushed and bruised below
Steel hooves and wounded men!
O tell, fair sorceress, tell if thou dost know.

This poor racked wretch the wolf already flays
O'er whom the vultures whirr,
This broken warrior! if in vain he prays
For cross and sepulchre.
This anguished wretch the wolf already flays!

How should we rend dense gulfs which know not dawn
Nor eve, nor any star?
How pierce with light skies which abyss-like yawn
When black as pitch they are?
How should we rend dense gulfs which know not dawn?

Hope glimmered in the windows of the Inn,
But Hope is dead for aye!
Moonless and rayless, can poor travellers win

To shelter from the way?
The Devil made dark the windows of the Inn!

Dost love the damned, adorable sorceress?
Dost know the smitten sore?
Dost know Remorse that, grim and pitiless,
Feeds at my heart's red core?
Dost love the damned, adorable sorceress?

My soul is prey to the Irreparable,
It gnaws with tooth accurst,
And, termite-like, the cunning spawn of hell
Mines the foundations first!
My soul is prey to the Irreparable!

II

Often within a theatre I have seen,
'Thwart the orchestral roar,
A dazzling Fairy stand in sudden sheen
Where all was gloom before!
Often within a theatre I have seen

A being made of light and gold and gauze
Fling Demons to their fate!
But on my heart's dark stage an endless pause
Is all, and I await
In vain, in vain the Spirit with wings of gauze!

[SIR JOHN SQUIRE]

LVI

Causerie

You are an autumn sky, suffused with rose . . .
Yet sadness rises in me like the sea,
And on my sombre lip, when it outflows,
Leaves its salt burning slime for memory.

Over my swooning breast your fingers stray;
In vain, alas! My breast is a void pit
Sacked by the tooth and claw of woman. Nay,
Seek not my heart; the beasts have eaten it!

My heart is as a palace plunderèd
By the wolves, wherein they gorge and rend and kill.
A perfume round thy naked throat is shed . . .

Beauty, strong scourge of souls, O work thy will!
Scorch with thy fiery eyes which shine like feasts
These shreds of flesh rejected by the beasts!

[SIR JOHN SQUIRE]

LVII

Autumn Song

I

Soon shall we drown in winter, dark and chill;
Farewell to fiery summer's fleeting suns!
I hear already through the court-yard grill
The fire-logs crash grimly on the stones.

And winter's horrors will invade my soul:
Gloom, wrath and hateful toil will be my lot,

And like the sun in his far hell, the Pole,
My heart will be a red and frozen clot.

I listen shuddering to each falling log,
As criminals 'neath rising gibbets cower.
And I succumb to that grim dialogue
As to a battering ram a crumbling tower;

Till in my dream the cradling echoes drum
Like frantic hammers finishing a bier.
For whom?—Last night was summer; now is come
October, and the parting of the year.

II

I love thy long green eyes of slumberous fire,
My sweet, but now all things are gall to me,
And naught, thy room, thy hearth nor thy desire
Is worth the sunlight shimmering on the sea.

Yet love me, tender heart! as mothers love
Even a thankless or a wicked son;
Mistress or sister, shed the glories of
A brief October or a setting sun.

'Twill not be long! The hungry tomb awaits!
Ah! Let me, forehead resting on thy knees,
Savour, regretful of the bleaching heats,
The amber glow of autumn's sorceries!

[LEWIS PIAGET SHANKS]

LVIII

To a Madonna

(AN EX-VOTO IN THE SPANISH TASTE)

Madonna, mistress, I would build for thee
An altar deep in the sad soul of me;
And in the darkest corner of my heart,
From mortal hopes and mocking eyes apart,
Carve of enamelled blue and gold a shrine
For thee to stand erect in, Image divine!
And with a mighty Crown thou shalt be crowned
Wrought of the gold of my smooth Verse, set round
With starry crystal rhymes; and I will make,
O mortal maid, a Mantle for thy sake,
And weave it of my jealousy, a gown
Heavy, barbaric, stiff, and weighted down
With my distrust, and broider round the hem
Not pearls, but all my tears in place of them.
And then thy wavering, trembling robe shall be
All the desires that rise and fall in me
From mountain-peaks to valleys of repose,
Kissing thy lovely body's white and rose.
For thy humiliated feet divine,
Of my Respect I'll make thee Slippers fine
Which, prisoning them within a gentle fold,
Shall keep their imprint like a faithful mould.
And if my art, unwearying and discreet,
Can make no Moon of Silver for thy feet
To have for Footstool, then thy heel shall rest
Upon the snake that gnaws within my breast,
Victorious Queen of whom our hope is born!
And thou shalt trample down and make a scorn
Of the vile reptile swollen up with hate.
And thou shalt see my thoughts, all consecrate,
Like candles set before thy flower-strewn shrine,
O Queen of Virgins, and the taper-shine
Shall glimmer star-like in the vault of blue,
With eyes of flame for ever watching you.

À
VNE DAME C...

Au pays parfumé que le soleil caress...
J'ai connu, sous un dais d'ar...
Et de palmiers d'où pleut sur les...
Une dame créole aux charmes igno...
Son teint est pâle et chaud ;
A dans le cou des airs noble...
Grande et svelte en marchant co...
Son sourire est tranquille ch...
Si vous alliez, Madame...
Sur les bords de la Seine...
Belle digne d'orner les antique...
Vous feriez, à l'abri des om...
Germer mille sonnets dans...
Que vos grands yeux rendra...
plus soumis...

OLE

~~t en pourprés~~
~~laresse,~~

che enchanteresse
nières;
e chasseresse,
ux assurés.
i pays de Gloire,
Belle Loire,
irs,
traites
un des poëtes

s noirs.

While all the love and worship in my sense
Will be sweet smoke of myrrh and frankincense.
Ceaselessly up to thee, white peak of snow,
My stormy spirit will in vapours go!

And last, to make thy drama all complete,
That love and cruelty may mix and meet,
I, thy remorseful torturer, will take
All the Seven Deadly Sins, and from them make
In darkest joy, Seven Knives, cruel-edged and keen,
And like a juggler choosing, O my Queen,
That spot profound whence love and mercy start,
I'll plunge them all within thy panting heart!

[JAMES HUNEKER]

LIX

An Afternoon Song

Little witch, with witching lashes,
Falling over witching eyes,
Tho' your glances scarcely tell me
Of an angel's chastest sighs—

I adore thee, in my passion,
Careless, thoughtless girl of mine,
With the priest's wild mad devotion
For his idol and his shrine.

Scents from desert, and from forest
Have embalm'd your wide-flung tresses,
And your head has all the movements
Of all secret, guessless guesses.

From your flesh the sweet faint odour,
Like some sacred incensed fume,
Rises till you charm like midnight,
Nymph of warmth and shady gloom!

All the strongest, wildest philtres
Are not worth your idle graces,
E'en dead corpses would revive them
Underneath your wild embraces.

Your soft white hips are amorous
Of your back and full, ripe breasts,
Like two hills of snow, rose-frozen,
With rose blossoms on their crests.

E'en the cushions throb with pleasure,
As your lazy form discloses
All the soft, voluptuous beauty
Of a thousand languid poses.

Sometimes to appease the passion
Of love's torments, love's delights,
You will flood my lips with kisses,
Tease my lips with pearly bites;

And then tear my soul out, darling,
With a peal of mocking laughter
Till, repentant, soft eyes steep them
In mine own a moment after.

Underneath your satin slippers
Have I thrown my love, my hate,
Have I flung my joy, my manhood,
Flung my genius and my fate!

Can you heal my soul, my darling,
You all colour, warmth and light?
Can you, sweet, dispel the darkness
Of my drear, Siberian night?

[HARRY CURWEN]

LX

Sisina

Think of Diana crashing through the wood,
Wind on her breast and in her tangled hair,
Beating the thicket, finding the tumult good,
The forest's pride, the swiftest steed's despair.

See, see Théroigne, thirsty for tyrant's blood,
Urging to war a troop whose feet are bare,
As, cheeks aflame, she stands where kings have stood,
And mounts, with sword in hand, the royal stair.

Such is Sisina! with a soul on fire,
But charity is mingled with her ire,
And her gay courage in the battle's heat

Lays down its arms to quiet the suppliant's fears,
And, when she sees the unhappy at her feet,
That flaming heart becomes a fount of tears.

[JAMES LAVER]

LXI

VERSES FOR THE PORTRAIT OF

Honoré Daumier

He whose image lights our page,
One whose art, a subtle elf,
Teaches man to laugh at self,
Reader, was a master-sage.

Jester he, ironic, tart;
But the force with which he shows
Evil, what from evil flows,
Proves the grace within his heart.

His no grin or venomous
Sneer of princes of the pit,
By Alecto's torches lit,
Firing them, but freezing us.

Theirs the laugh of merriment
Woeful, painful travesty;
Radiant his, large, frank and free,
Pledge of pow'r beneficent!

[ARTHUR ELLIS]

LXII

Franciscae Meae Laudes

VERSES WRITTEN FOR A LEARNED AND PIOUS DRESSMAKER

Songs from mine exasperation
Dear girl, lithe-limbed, of my creation,
In heart's solitude's crispation.

This intricately disseminated,
A woman too delicate to be hated,
Who saves our souls our God created!

As in Lethe fulminated,
I shall drain your kisses violated
In your magnetism impregnated.

When the tempest of our Vices
Shall shatter the shrines of sacrifices,
Lo, the Divinity swathed in spices,

As the sailor's star that hovers
Over many sleepless lovers
I shall hang my heart on shrines she covers.

Well-water that is full of virtue,
Eternal spring of youth desert you
Never while my kisses hurt you!

What was soiled, burn with aspersion;
What was ribald, to wrath's reversion;
What was nerveless, to hell's perversion!

For my hunger, tavern-raven,
Light my midnight, cavern-paven,
With hell's perils straight to haven.

Add to venom venomous,
Scented breath, male, odorous,
Senses strange and savourous!

My lean languid limbs set quivering
No chaste hints of your delivering,
Water dyed from pinions shivering:

Golden jewels coruscated,
Salt bread, Francisca, never tasted,
Divine wine on your beauty wasted!

[ARTHUR SYMONS]

LXIII

Sonnet

(TO A CREOLE LADY)

In far south lands made sweet with fragrant balms
I knew, beneath the shade of purpled trees
And drowsy stillness of the drooping palms,
Afar from towns, withdrawn in slothful ease,
A Creole lady. Pale her tint, but warm,
With soft brown skin, and nobly carried head,
With tranquil smile, and dainty slender form,
Assured calm eyes, and supple springy tread.

If ever, madam, fate shall shape your ways
To glorious France, your grace—which nothing lacks
To flash the jewel of some ancient seat—
Within the shadows of your sure retreat
Will cause a thousand sonnets in its praise,
And make our hearts more humble than your blacks.

[EUGENE MASON]

LXIV

Mœsta et Errabunda

Say, Agatha, dost thou in dreams delight
— Far from the city's black and filthy sea —
To rove where other oceans burst in light,
Blue, deep, and crystal-clear as chastity?
Say, Agatha, dost thou in dreams delight?

The mighty ocean is our comforter!
What demon gave the sea, contralto hoarse,
— And the harsh winds' vast organ made for her —
The lofty notes that lull a soul's remorse?
The mighty ocean is our comforter!

Bear me away, swift car and frigate white!
Afar! — afar! this mud is made of tears!
— Agatha, truly does thy heart recite
In sadness: Far from crime, remorse and fears,
Bear me away, swift car and frigate white?

How far away that fragrant Eden lies,
Those clear blue skies where love and joy allure,
Where all we love is worthy, — paradise
Where spirits drown in calm delights and pure!
How far away that fragrant Eden lies!

But the green Eden of our youthful loves,
Songs, races, roses, kisses all athrill,
The jugs of wine, at dusk, in shadowy groves,
The quivering violins beyond the hill,
— But the green Eden of our youthful loves,

Our Eden of pure tremulous ecstasies,
Is it now farther than the shores of Ind?
Can tears or cries recall its sorceries,
Or prayers or silvery words some evening find
Our Eden of pure tremulous ecstasies?

[LEWIS PIAGET SHANKS]

LXV

The Ghostly Visitant

Like the mild-eyed angels sweet
I will come to thy retreat,
Stealing in without a sound
When the shades of night close round.

I will give thee manifold
Kisses soft and moony-cold,
Gliding, sliding o'er thee like
A serpent crawling round a dike.

When the livid morn creeps on
You will wake and find me gone
Till the evening come again.

As by tenderness and ruth
Others rule thy life and youth,
I by terror choose to reign.

[SIR JOHN SQUIRE]

LXVI

Sonnet of Autumn

They say to me, thy clear and crystal eyes:
'Why dost thou love me so, strange lover mine?'
Be sweet, be still! My heart and soul despise
All save that antique brute-like faith of thine;

And will not bare the secret of their shame
To thee whose hand soothes me to slumbers long,
Nor their black legend write for thee in flame!
Passion I hate, a spirit does me wrong.

Let us love gently. Love, from his retreat,
Ambushed and shadowy, bends his fatal bow,
And I too well his ancient arrows know:

Crime, horror, folly. O pale marguerite,
Thou art as I, a bright sun fallen low,
O my so white, my so cold Marguerite.

[JAMES HUNEKER]

LXVII

The Sadness of the Moon

This evening the Moon dreams more languidly,
Like a beauty who on many cushions rests,
And with her light hand fondles lingeringly,
Before she sleeps, the slope of her sweet breasts.

On her soft satined avalanches' height
Dying, she laps herself for hours and hours
In long, long swoons, and gazes at the white
Visions which rise athwart the blue-like flowers.

When sometimes in her perfect indolence
She lets a furtive tear steal gently thence,
Some pious poet, a lone, sleepless one,

Takes in his hollowed hand this gem, shot through,
Like an opal stone, with gleams of every hue,
And in his heart's depths hides it from the sun.

[SIR JOHN SQUIRE]

LXVIII

The Cats

The lover and the stern philosopher
Both love, in their ripe time, the confident
Soft cats, the house's chiefest ornament,
Who like themselves are cold and seldom stir.

Of knowledge and of pleasure amorous,
Silence they seek and Darkness' fell domain;
Had not their proud souls scorned to brook his rein,
They would have made grim steeds for Erebus.

Pensive they rest in noble attitudes
Like great stretched sphinxes in vast solitudes
Which seem to sleep wrapt in an endless dream;

Their fruitful loins are full of sparks divine,
And gleams of gold within their pupils shine
As 'twere within the shadow of a stream.

[SIR JOHN SQUIRE]

LXIX

The Owls

The owls that roost in the black yew
Along one limb in solemn state,
And with a red eye look you through,
Are eastern gods; they meditate.

No feather stirs on them, not one,
Until that melancholy hour
When night, supplanting the weak sun,
Resumes her interrupted power.

Their attitude instructs the wise
To shun all action, all surprise.
Suppose there passed a lovely face, —

Who even longs to follow it,
Must feel for ever the disgrace
Of having all but moved a bit.

[EDNA ST. VINCENT MILLAY]

LXX

The Pipe

An author's favourite pipe am I,
My Kaffir woman's countenance
Tells the beholder at a glance
My master smokes incessantly.

If he is mournful or in pain
I smoke as does the ploughman's cot
When the good wife prepares the pot
Before her spouse comes home again.

I bind his soul and rock her well
In the blue twisting skein which slips
And rises from my fiery lips,

And weave a very potent spell
Which soothes his heart in its distress
And heals his spirit's weariness.

[SIR JOHN SQUIRE]

LXXI

Music

Oft Music, as it were some moving mighty sea,
Bears me toward my pale
Star: in clear space, or 'neath a vaporous canopy
On-floating, I set sail.

With heaving chest which strains forward, and
    lungs outblown,
I climb the ridgèd steeps
Of those high-pilèd clouds which 'thwart the night
    are thrown,
Veiling its starry deeps.

I suffer all the throes, within my quivering form,
Of a great ship in pain,
Now a soft wind, and now the writhings of a storm

Upon the vasty main
Rock me: at other times a death-like calm, the bare
Mirror of my despair.

[SIR JOHN SQUIRE]

LXXII

The Burial of the Accursed

If haply one dark, dreary night
Some charitable soul appear
And 'neath old rubble stow from sight
The body that you held so dear —

What time the chaste stars veil their eyes,
Drowsy and fain for slumber, there
Spiders shall weave their traceries,
Vipers their spotted young shall bear.

Above your doomed head you will hear
Each night throughout the heavy year
The lean wolves' melancholy cries,

Famished hags' howlings for a crust,
Lewd pastimes of old men who lust,
And scoundrels' dark conspiracies.

[SIR JOHN SQUIRE]

LXXIII

A Fantastic Engraving

This strange, gaunt spectre nothing wears at all
Save, on his head, a crown of Carnival,
Grotesquely perched upon his naked skull.
Without or whip or spur (its nostrils full
Of dribbling foam) he urges on its course
His ghastly, grim, Apocalyptic horse,
And horse and rider, through a space as wide
As is Infinity, tumultuous ride.

And while his mount treads down a nameless horde,
The spectral rider shakes his flaming sword
Over the mighty, royal realm that is
His broad estate — one vast necropolis,
Where sleep, beneath the cold sun's joyless eye,
All the inhabitants of History.

[JAMES LAVER]

LXXIV

The Joyous Corse

In a soil full of snails and free from stones
I fain would dig myself a pit full deep,
Where I might lay at ease my agèd bones
And, like a wave-borne shark, forgetful sleep.

For testaments I hate, and tombs I hate;
Rather than crave a tear from human eyes
I would invite the crows their hunger sate
Upon my corpse's foul extremities.

O worms! O black, deaf, sightless company!
There comes to you a dead man glad and free.
O philosophic sons of rottenness,
Across my ruin crawl without remorse,
And tell if any pain may yet oppress
This old and soulless death-surrounded corse.

[SIR JOHN SQUIRE]

LXXV

The Barrel of Hatred

Hate is the barrel of the pale Danaides;
Vengeance with enormous arms utterly frantic
Precipitates into the void darkness of the Seas
Huge buckets full of blood and of snakes that antic.

The Demon in his abysses has made secret hollows
Through which fly sweating more than a thousand years,
After his heedless victims Hate hastily follows,
Makes bleed their bodies, galvanized by his shears.

Hate is a drunkard at the far end of a Tavern,
Who feels always his intense thirst born of his drink
Multiply himself like a hydra in a Cavern.

— But the jolly drunkards know to what depths they sink,
And that Hate endures this pang redoubtable
Of never having slept even in Hell.

[ARTHUR SYMONS]

LXXVI

The Cracked Bell

'Tis bitter-sweet, when winter nights are long,
To watch, beside the flames which smoke and twist,
The distant memories which slowly throng,
Brought by the chime soft-singing through the mist.

Happy the sturdy, vigorous-throated bell
Who, spite of age alert and confident,
Cries hourly, like some strong old sentinel
Flinging the ready challenge from his tent.

For me, my soul is cracked; when, sick with care,
She strives with songs to people the cold air
It happens often that her feeble cries

Mock the harsh rattle of a man who lies
Wounded, forgotten, 'neath a mound of slain
And dies, pinned fast, writhing his limbs in vain.

[SIR JOHN SQUIRE]

LXXVII

Spleen

November, angry at the capital,
Whelms in a death-chill from her gloomy urn
The pallid dead beneath the grave-yard wall,
The death-doomed who in dripping houses yearn.

Grimalkin prowls, a gaunt and scurvy ghoul,
Seeking a softer spot for her sojourn;
Under the eaves an ancient poet's soul
Shivers and flees and wails at each return.

The grieving church-bell and the sputtering log
Repeat the rusty clock's harsh epilogue;
While in a pack of cards, scent-filled and vile,

Grim relic of a spinster dropsical,
The knave of hearts and queen of spades recall
Their loves defunct, and sinistrously smile.

[LEWIS PIAGET SHANKS]

LXXVIII

The Sphinx

I swear to you that if I lived a thousand years
I could not be more crammed with dubious souvenirs.

There's no old chest of drawers bulging with deeds
    and bills,
Love-letters, locks of hair, novels, bad verses, wills,
That hides so many secrets as my wretched head; —
It's like a mausoleum, like a pyramid,
Holding more heaped unpleasant bones than
    Potter's Field;
I am a graveyard hated by the moon; revealed
Never by her blue light are those long worms that force
Into my dearest dead their blunt snouts of remorse.
— I am an old boudoir, where roses dried and brown
Have given their dusty odour to the faded gown,
To the ridiculous hat, doubtless in other days
So fine, among the wan pastels and pale Bouchers.

Time has gone lame, and limps; and under a thick pall
Of snow the endless years efface and muffle all;
Till boredom, fruit of the mind's inert, incurious tree,
Assumes the shape and size of immortality.

Henceforth, O living matter, you are nothing more
Than the fixed heart of chaos, soft horror's granite core,
Than a forgotten Sphinx that in some desert stands,
Drowsing beneath the heat, half-hidden by the sands,
Unmarked on any map, — whose rude and sullen frown
Lights up a moment only when the sun goes down.

[EDNA ST. VINCENT MILLAY]

Rien ne peut l'égayer,

ni Gibier

ni faucon,

Ni son peuple mourant

en face du balcon

Du bouffon favori

la grotesque ball

Ne distrait plus le front

de ce cruel malade,

LXXIX

The King of the Rainy Country

A rainy country this, that I am monarch of, —
A rich but powerless king, worn-out while yet a boy;
For whom in vain the falcon falls upon the dove;
Not even his starving people's groans can give him joy;
Scorning his tutors, loathing his spaniels, finding stale
His favourite jester's quips, yawning at the droll tale.
His bed, for all its *fleurs de lis*, looks like a tomb;
The ladies of the court, attending him, to whom
He, being a prince, is handsome, see him lying there
Cold as a corpse, and lift their shoulders in despair:
No garment they take off, no garter they leave on
Excites the gloomy eye of this young skeleton.
The royal alchemist, who makes him gold from lead,
The baser element from out the royal head
Cannot extract; nor can those Roman baths of blood,
For some so efficacious, cure the hebetude
Of him, along whose veins, where flows no blood at all,
For ever the slow waters of green Lethe crawl.

[EDNA ST. VINCENT MILLAY]

LXXX

Spleen

When the low heavy sky weighs like a lid
Upon the spirit aching for the light,
And all the wide horizon's line is hid
By a black day sadder than any night;

When the changed earth is but a dungeon dank
Where batlike Hope goes blindly fluttering
And, striking wall and roof and mouldered plank,
Bruises his tender head and timid wing;

When like grim prison-bars stretch down the thin,
Straight, rigid pillars of the endless rain,
And the dumb throngs of infamous spiders spin
Their meshes in the caverns of the brain; —

Suddenly, bells leap forth into the air,
Hurling a hideous uproar to the sky
As 'twere a band of homeless spirits who fare
Through the strange heavens, wailing stubbornly.

And hearses, without drum or instrument,
File slowly through my soul; crushed, sorrowful,
Weeps Hope, and Grief, fierce and omnipotent,
Plants his black banner on my drooping skull.

[SIR JOHN SQUIRE]

LXXXI

Obsession

As though within a vast cathedral dim,
Great woods, I shudder at your organ-groan!
Our wrung hearts answer with a desperate hymn
The unending *De Profundis* you intone.
Ocean, I hate your truceless tides that own
A likeness to my spirit! and the grim
Enormous laughter of your waters blown
Above man's bitter doom, deriding him!

But thee I love, O Night when no stars spell
The speech of Light's reverberate syllable
To one who seeks the void, the dark, the unknown!
Each cloud's a tent upon the field of night
Where, thousands upon thousands in pure light,
Dwell once familiar beings who have flown!

[WILFRID THORLEY]

LXXXII

Annihilation

Poor weary soul! To think how thou wouldst plunge
   and leap
When the bright spur of Hope into thy flank was pressed!
He has unsaddled thee for good. Lie down and rest,
Old spavined horse, old nag not worthy of thy keep.

Thou, too, my heart, lie down and sleep thy bestial sleep.

And thou, my mind, old highwayman, thou who
   didst fling
Thyself from ambush upon every joy, go thou
And skulk in peace. No pleasure will come near thee now;
No joy can tempt so sombre and uncouth a thing.

Gone, gone: even that infallible sweet thrill of spring!

Time blots me out, as flakes on freezing bodies fall;
I see the whole round world, with every animal,
And every flower, and every leaf on every branch,
And there is absolutely nothing I like at all.

Come down and carry me away, O avalanche.

[GEORGE DILLON]

LXXXIII

The Alchemy of Grief

One, Nature! burns and makes thee bright,
One gives thee weeds to mourn withal;
And what to one is burial
Is to the other life and light.

The unknown Hermes who assists
And always fills my heart with fear,
Makes the mighty Midas' peer
The saddest of the alchemists.

Through him I make gold changeable
To dross, and paradise to hell;
Clouds for its corpse-cloths I descry.

A stark dead body I love well,
And in the gleaming fields on high
I build immense sarcophagi.

[SIR JOHN SQUIRE]

LXXXIV

Magnetic Horror

'From this bizarre and livid sky
Tormented like your doom and mine,
On your void spirit passing by,
What thoughts descend, O libertine?'

— Athirst for mortal things unsung,
In shadowy realms of lone surmise,
I will not whine like Ovid, flung
From out the Latin paradise.

Skies torn like strands of ocean-streams,
In you is mirrored all my pride!
Your slow, enormous clouds abide

The dolent hearses of my dreams;
Your glimmers mock with fluctuant lights
The hell wherein my heart delights.

[CLARK ASHTON SMITH]

LXXXV

The Peace-Pipe

On the Mountains of the Prairie,
On the great Red Pipe-stone Quarry,
Gitche Manito, the mighty,
He the Master of Life, descending,
On the red crags of the quarry
Stood erect, and called the nations,
Called the tribes of men together.

From the red stone of the quarry
With his hand he broke a fragment,
Moulded it into a pipe-head,
Shaped and fashioned it with figures;
From the margin of the river
Took a long reed for a pipe-stem,
With its dark green leaves upon it;
Filled the pipe with bark of willow,
With the bark of the red willow;
Breathed upon the neighbouring forest,
Made its great boughs chafe together,
Till in flame they burst and kindled;
And erect upon the mountains,

Gitche Manito, the mighty,
Smoked the calumet, the Peace-Pipe,
As a signal to the nations.

And the smoke rose slowly, slowly,
Through the tranquil air of morning,
First a single line of darkness,
Then a denser, bluer vapour,
Then a snow-white cloud unfolding,
Like the tree-tops of the forest,
Ever rising, rising, rising,
Till it touched the top of heaven,
Till it broke against the heaven,
And rolled outward all around it.

From the Vale of Tawasentha,
From the Valley of Wyoming,
From the groves of Tuscaloosa,
From the far-off Rocky Mountains,
From the Northern lakes and rivers,
All the tribes beheld the signal,
Saw the distant smoke ascending,
The Pukwana of the Peace-Pipe.

And the Prophets of the nations
Said: 'Behold it, the Pukwana!
By this signal from afar off,
Bending like a wand of willow,
Waving like a hand that beckons,
Gitche Manito, the mighty,
Calls the tribes of men together,
Calls the warriors to his council!'

Down the rivers, o'er the prairies,
Came the warriors of the nations,
All the warriors drawn together
By the signal of the Peace-Pipe,
To the Mountains of the Prairie,
To the great Red Pipe-stone Quarry.

And they stood there on the meadow,
With their weapons and their war-gear,
Painted like the leaves of Autumn,
Painted like the sky of morning,
Wildly glaring at each other;
In their faces stern defiance,
In their hearts the feuds of ages,
The hereditary hatred,
The ancestral thirst of vengeance.

Gitche Manito, the mighty,
The creator of the nations,
Looked upon them with compassion,
With paternal love and pity;
Looked upon their wrath and wrangling
But as quarrels among children,
But as feuds and fights of children!

Over them he stretched his right hand,
To subdue their stubborn natures,
To allay their thirst and fever,
By the shadow of his right hand;
Spake to them with voice majestic
As the sound of far-off waters
Falling into deep abysses,
Warning, chiding, spake in this wise: —

'O my children! my poor children!
Listen to the words of wisdom,
Listen to the words of warning,
From the lips of the Great Spirit,
From the Master of Life who made you!

'I have given you lands to hunt in,
I have given you streams to fish in,
I have given you bear and bison,
I have given you roe and reindeer,
I have given you brant and beaver,
Filled the marshes full of wild fowl,

Filled the rivers full of fishes;
Why then are you not contented?
Why then will you hunt each other?

'I am weary of your quarrels,
Weary of your wars and bloodshed,
Weary of your prayers for vengeance,
Of your wranglings and dissensions;
All your strength is in your union,
All your danger is in discord;
Therefore be at peace henceforward,
And as brothers live together.

'I will send a Prophet to you,
A Deliverer of the nations,
Who shall guide you and shall teach you,
Who shall toil and suffer with you.
If you listen to his counsels,
You will multiply and prosper;
If his warnings pass unheeded,
You will fade away and perish!

'Bathe now in the stream before you,
Wash the war-paint from your faces,
Wash the blood-stains from your fingers,
Bury your war-clubs and your weapons,
Break the red stone from this quarry,
Mould and make it into Peace-Pipes,
Take the reeds that grow beside you,
Deck them with your brightest feathers,
Smoke the calumet together,
And as brothers live henceforward!'

Then upon the ground the warriors
Threw their cloaks and shirts of deer-skin,
Threw their weapons and their war-gear,
Leaped into the rushing river,
Washed the war-paint from their faces.

And in silence all the warriors
Broke the red stone of the quarry,
Smoothed and formed it into Peace-Pipes,
Broke the long reeds by the river,
Decked them with their brightest feathers,
And departed each one homeward,
While the Master of Life ascending,
Through the opening of cloud-curtains,
Through the doorways of the heaven,
Vanished from before their faces,
In the smoke that rolled around him,
The Pukwana of the Peace-Pipe!

[HENRY WADSWORTH LONGFELLOW]

LXXXVI

The Pagan's Prayer

Ah, damp not yet the living coals!
Heat once again my heart in thee!
Voluptuousness, thou scourge of souls,
Goddess, incline thine ear to me!

Spirit abroad in the bright air,
Flame in our dark and secret ways,
Freezing I bring thee—grant my prayer!—
A song of brass to bruit thy praise!

Siren, be still my sovereign; keep
Thy kingdom; wear thy mask, whose mesh
Is half of velvet, half of flesh!

Or pour me out thy heavy sleep,
In mystic and amorphous wine:
Phantom elastic and divine.

[EDNA ST. VINCENT MILLAY]

LXXXVII

The Lid

Where'er he wings his way o'er land and sea,
'Neath skies of flame or where pale suns gleam white,
Whether Christ or Venus holds his heart in fee,
Be he beggar lone or Croesus golden bright,

In field or city, clerk or wanderer free,
If slow his little mind or keen and light,
Man ever feels the fear of mystery's might
And always looks he skyward tremblingly.

Skyward to Heaven! The cave wall stifling day,
The lighted ceiling of a comic play,
Where every actor falls in the silly strife!

Hope of mad hermits, fear of the rakes who scoff,
Heaven, the black lid of the mighty trough,
Where drinks the shadowy mass of human life!

[EDWARD H. LASCELLES]

LXXXVIII

The Unforeseen

Harpagon, sitting up beside his father's bed,
Mused, as the breathing altered and the lips went grey,
'I've plenty of old planks, I think, out in the shed;
I saw them there the other day.'

Célimène coos and says, 'How beautiful I am!
God, since my heart is kind, has made me fair, as well!'
Her heart!—as tough as leather, her heart!—smoked like
    a ham;
And turning on a spit in hell!

A sputtering gazetteer, who thinks he casts a light,
Says to his readers drowned in paradox and doubt,
'Where do you see him, then, this God of Truth
  and Right?
This Saviour that you talk about?'

Better than these I know—although I know all three—
That foppish libertine, who yawns in easy grief
Nightly upon my shoulder, 'All right, you wait and see;
I'm turning over a new leaf!'

The clock says, 'The condemned is ready; you may call
For him; I have advised in vain as to those flaws
Which threatened; Man is blind, deaf, fragile—
  like a wall
In which an insect lives and gnaws.'

Whereat a Presence, stranger to few, greeted by none,
Appears. 'Well met!' he mocks; 'have I not seen you pass
Before my sacred vessel, in communion
Of joyousness, at the Black Mass?

'Each of you builds in secret a temple to my fame;
Each one of you in secret has kissed my foul behind;
Look at me; hear this laughter: *Satan* is my name,—
Lewd, monstrous as the world! Oh, blind,

'Oh, hypocritical men!—and did you think indeed
To mock your master?—trick him till double wage
  be given?
Did it seem likely two such prizes be decreed:
To be so rich—and enter Heaven?

'The game must pay the hunter; the hunter for his prey
Lies chilled and cramped so long behind the vain decoy;
Down through the thickness now I carry you away,
Companions of my dreary joy;

'Down through the thickness of primeval earth and rock,
Thickness of human ashes helter-skelter blown,
Into a palace huge as I,—a single block—
And of no soft and crumbling stone!—

'For it is fashioned whole from Universal Sin;
And it contains my grief, my glory and my pride!'
—Meantime, from his high perch above our earthly din,
An Angel sounds the victory wide

Of those whose heart says, 'Blessèd be this punishment,
O Lord! O Heavenly Father, be this anguish blest!
My soul in Thy kind hands at last is well content,
A toy no more; Thou knowest best!'

So sweetly, so deliciously that music flows
Through the cool harvest evenings of these celestial days,
That like an ecstasy it penetrates all those
Of whose pure lives it sings the praise.

[EDNA ST. VINCENT MILLAY]

LXXXIX

Self-Questioning at Midnight

The pendulum, with brazen din,
Proclaims the midnight; we begin
To call to mind, ironically,
What uses we have made of this
Dead day that drops to the abyss:
To-day, O, date prophetical,
Friday thirteenth, in sombre folly
Maugre the truth our heart maintains,
We, seeing still the light that sains,
Have walked in ways heretical.

We have blasphemed the might of Jesus,
The most irrefutable Lord;
And like a parasite at the board
Of some abominable Croesus,
To please the monstrous animal,
True servitor of Asmodai,
We have denied and flouted all
The things we love eternally,
And all the things that we despise
Greeted with slavish flattery;

A servile executioner,
Bemoaned the wrong of our mesprise;
Bowed to immense Stupidity,
Stupidity the minotaur;
Kissed with devotion prodigal
The brainless Matter's red and white,
And praised the dim phosphoric light
That is corruption's final pall.

Likewise, to drown the vertigo
Of vision, dream and dolour febrile,
We, the proud servant of the Lyre,
The Lyre, whose glow is to show
The drunkenness of things funebral,
Again have drunk with no desire,
Have eaten still with no delight. . . .
Swiftly blow out the lamp, for we
Would shroud us in the secrecy
And dark indifference of Night!

[CLARK ASHTON SMITH]

XC

A Mournful Madrigal

Ah, what to me though you be wise,
So you be fair, so you be sad?
Tears lend allurement to your eyes,
For streams are sweet where'er they rise:
Storms make the drooping blossoms glad.

I love you best when all delight
Down from your darkening brow is cast,
When your heart drowns in horror's night,
When all is blotted from your sight
By direful clouds from out the past.

I love you when your wide eyes weep
A water warm as though 'twere blood,
When, whilst my hand would bring you sleep,
You cry aloud in anguish deep
As though death bore you towards his flood.

Like to celestial harmonies
Profound, voluptuous, apart,
I breathe your sobbing agonies,
And watch the pearls that dewed your eyes
Shedding their gleam within your heart.

Your heart wherein, though dispossessed,
Shadows of outworn loves are tossed,
Flames on with forge-like, fierce unrest,
The while you nurture in your breast
Some of the pride that haunts the lost.

Yet in so far, love, as your dream
Never has plunged you deep as hell,
Since ne'er, on nightmare's eddying stream
Where lust is hot for weapon's gleam,
For powder's havoc, poison's spell,

Where all men are shut out as foes,
Evil is read in every fate,
Where, shuddering, chimes each hour that goes,
Have you felt all about you close
The clutch of comprehensive Hate;

Therefore, my slave-queen, you may not,
Who mix with fear love's offering,
Tell me amid night's noisome blot
With urgent clamour heart-begot
'I am your equal, O my King!'

[DOROTHY MARTIN]

XCI

The Fang

Each man who is a man can show
A yellow Serpent in his heart,
Installed as on a throne apart,
That cries to all his wishes: 'No!'

Plunge in the fixed and frozen lies
Of Satyr-maids' or Nixies' eyes,
The Fang says: 'Duty, not Delight!'

Beget thee sons, or plant a tree,
Carve blocks of marble, poetry,
The Fang says: 'If thou die to-night?'

Whatever plan or hope we grasp
We cannot live one moment and
Escape the warning reprimand
Of that intolerable asp.

[LEWIS PIAGET SHANKS]

XCII

To a Girl from Malabar

Your feet and hands are delicate, your thighs
No European beauty dare despise,
Nor artist fail to find delight therein.
Your eyes are darker velvet than your skin.
In those hot, purple lands, your native soil,
To light your master's pipe was all your toil,
To bring sweet scents and water cold as snow,
And chase away the roving mosquito.
And, when the morning makes the plane-trees sing,
Forth for ripe fruits to fare a-marketing,
Bare-footed, at your will, roam here and there,
And sing, all day, some old, forgotten air.
And when the night descends with cloak of red,
On a bare mat to make your easy bed,
Where flits the humming-bird before closed eyes,
And dreams are but another Paradise.
Why come you here, O child of careless hours,
To this unhappy, crowded land of ours,
Why to a sailor that dark beauty sell,
And to your tamarinds bid a long farewell?
Half-naked underneath your muslin dress,
And shivering in our Winter's bitterness,
How, as the cruel corset cramps your blood,
And for your food you forage in the mud
That fills our gutters, you will pine and weep
To sell the scent of your strange beauty cheap,
And through our dark fogs strive in vain to find
The ghostly palm-trees you have left behind.

[JAMES LAVER]

XCIII

The Voice

I grew up in the shadow of a big bookcase: a tall
Babel, where verses, novels, histories, row upon row—
The immemorial ashes of Greek and Latin—all
Mingled and murmured. When I was as high as a folio,
I heard two voices speaking. The first one said: 'Be wise;
The world is but a large, delicious cake, my friend!
It calls for an appetite of corresponding size—
And whoso heeds my counsel, his joys shall have no end.'
The other voice spoke softly: 'Come, travel with me
 in dreams,
Far, far beyond the range of the possible and the known!'
And in that voice was the senseless music of winds
 and streams
Blown suddenly out of nowhere and into
 nowhere blown—
A phantom cry, a sound to frighten and captivate.
And I replied: 'I will, O lovely voice!' And from
That hour was sealed for ever the disastrous fate
Which still attends me: Always, behind the tedium
Of finite semblances, beyond the accustomed zone
Of time and space, I see distinctly another world—
And I must wear with loathing these mortal toils, as one
Dragging a weight of serpents about his ankles curled.
And from that hour, like the old prophets of Palestine,
I love extravagantly the wilderness and the sea;
I find an ineffable joy in the taste of harsh, sour wine;
I smile at the saddest moments; I weep amid gaiety;
I take facts for illusions—and often as not, with my eyes
Fixed confidently upon the heavens, I fall into holes.
But the Voice comforts me: 'Guard, fool, thy dreams!
 The wise
Have none so beautiful as thou hast.' And the
 Voice consoles.

[GEORGE DILLON]

XCIV

Agnostos Theos

Lovely and loved, by whose light shine
Our lights, the spiritual eye,
To thee, Life's Angel, and Divine
Idea, be immortality!

Like airs whose salt makes sickness whole,
Through all my powers thy power spreads,
And on my never-satiate soul
The zest of life Eternal sheds.

O scent of roses still perfuming
The lorn hold of thine anchorite,
Forgotten censer still reluming
The secret silences of night!

How may my lips, O Love, unblamed,
Thy life express that cannot lie?
Seed shaping, hid and half-ashamed,
That all of me that cannot die!

Lovely and loved, in whose joy mine,
And in thy health my health, must lie.
To thee, Life's Angel, and Divine
Idea, be immortality!

[H. W. GARROD]

XCV

The Rebel

An angel, like an eagle swept by wrath,
Drops earthward, plucks the sinner's hair full hard,
And cries: 'Thou shalt walk in a righteous path!
I will it, I who have thy soul in ward.
Know then that thou shalt love thy fellows, yea!
Knave, dolt, or misbegotten. Even thus
Thou shalt with charity make thy Lord's way,
When that He passeth by thee, glorious.

'Such is true Love. Ere thy hot blood turn chill,
Drink of the glory of God's burning grace
Wherein is a delight Time cannot kill.'
And the great Angel's giant arms apace
Smite down on the damned soul's defiant face
That yet doth answer: 'Nay, I never will!'

[WILFRID THORLEY]

XCVI

Bertha's Eyes

The loveliest eyes you can scorn with your wondrous glow:
O! beautiful childish eyes, there abounds in your light
A something unspeakably tender and good as the night:
O eyes! over me your enchanting darkness let flow.

Large eyes of my child! O Arcana profoundly adored!
Ye resemble so closely those caves in the magical creek;
Where within the deep slumbering shade of some
    petrified peak,
There shines, undiscovered, the gems of a dazzling hoard.

My child has got eyes so profound and so dark and so vast,
Like thee! O unending Night, and thy mystical shine:
Their flames are those thoughts that with Love and with
    Faith combine,
And sparkle deep down in the depths so alluring or chaste.

[CYRIL SCOTT]

XCVII

The Fountain

Thine eyes are heavy. Let them close.
Lie without opening them. Lie
Still in the lovely thoughtless pose
Where pleasure found thee. The long cry
Of moonlit waters that caress
The evening, languorous as thou art,
Lives on: So does the tenderness
Love has awakened in my heart.

    The fountain leaps and flowers
    In many roses,
    Whereon the moonlight flares.
    Their crystal petals, falling,
    Falling for ever,
    Are changèd to bright tears.

Even thus thy spirit, briefly lit
With the strange lightnings of desire,
Once more into the infinite
Flings up its pure forgetful fire,
As if the dusty earth to flee—
And blossoms there, and breaks apart,
And falls, and flows invisibly
Into the deep night of my heart.

The fountain leaps and flowers
In many roses,
Whereon the moonlight flares.
Their crystal petals, falling,
Falling for ever,
Are changèd to bright tears.

O thou, so fair and so forlorn,
How sweet, my lips upon thy breast,
To hear within its marble urn
The water sobbing without rest.
O moon, loud water, lovely night,
O leaves where the soft winds upstart,
O wild and melancholy light,
Ye are the image of my heart.

The fountain leaps and flowers
In many roses,
Whereon the moonlight flares.
Their crystal petals, falling,
Falling for ever,
Are changèd to bright tears.

[GEORGE DILLON]

XCVIII

The Ransom

To pay his ransom man must toil
With Reason's implement alone
To plough and rake and free from stone
Two plots of hard volcanic soil.

And if he would from out them wrench
A few thorns or a meagre flower,
Continually a heavy shower
Of his salt sweat their roots must drench.

The one is Art, the other Love;
And on that last and terrible day
The wrath of the stern judge to stay
And 'scape the vengeance from above,

He must show barns whose uttermost
Recesses swell with ripened grain,
And blooms whose shapes and hues will gain
The suffrage of the Heavenly Host.

[SIR JOHN SQUIRE]

XCIX

Ever So Far from Here

Here is the chamber consecrate,
Wherein this maiden delicate,
And enigmatically sedate,

Fans herself while the moments creep,
Upon her cushions half-asleep,
And hears the fountains plash and weep:

Dorothy's chamber undefiled.
The winds and waters sing afar
Their song of sighing strange and wild
To lull to sleep the petted child.

From head to foot with subtle care,
Slaves have perfumed her delicate skin
With odorous oils and benzoin.
And flowers faint in a corner there.

[JAMES HUNEKER]

C

The Sundown of Romanticism

How goodly is the sun's first frank, resplendent beam,
When, with a burst of light, he throws us his 'Good-day!'
And happy he who can with love his setting ray
Salute, his setting ray more glorious than a dream!

I mind me to have seen all, field, flower, furrow, stream,
Throb like a fluttering heart, beneath the flooding sun.
Toward th' horizon, come, 'tis late, quick! let us run,
So at the least we may catch some last slanting gleam!

But I in vain pursue the God that sinks in death;
Th' inevitable Night its realm establisheth,
Black, humid, sinister and full of shadows grim.

Out of the darknesses a grave-like breath exhales
And my shy feet impinge, along the marish-rim,
On unexpected toads and cold and slimy snails.

[JOHN PAYNE]

CI

On the 'Tasso in Prison' of Eugène Delacroix

The poet in his cell, dishevell'd, white,
With foot convuls'd twisting a fallen scroll,
Measures with stare afire with mad affright
Rungs of the dizzying trance which gulfs his soul.

The wildering laughs which throng his prison-house,
Lure on his reason to the weird and absurd;
Doubts compass him about—wild fears begird,
Witless and multiform and hideous.

In hovel foul this genius confin'd,
These ghosts, cries, leers, aswarm, by spectral calls
Hallooed to swoop and whirl behind his ear,

This dreamer wak'd by his lodging's horror, here
Self's emblem, thou vague, visionary mind,
That the Real suffocates 'tween its four walls.

[ARTHUR ELLIS]

CII

The Pit

Great Pascal had his pit always in sight.
All is abysmal—deed, desire, or dream
Or speech! Full often over me doth scream
The wind of Fear and blows my hair upright.
By the lone strand, thro' silence, depth and height,
And shoreless space that doth with terrors teem . . .
On my black nights God's finger like a beam
Traces his swarming torments infinite.

Sleep is a monstrous hole that I do dread,
Full of vague horror, leading none knows where;
All windows open on infinity,
So that my dizzy spirit in despair
Longs for the torpor of the unfeeling dead.
Ah! from Time's menace never to win free!

[WILFRID THORLEY]

CIII

The Lament of Icarus

The customers of Love debased
Seem happy, calm and satisfied.
My arms hang limply by my side
Because I have a cloud embraced.

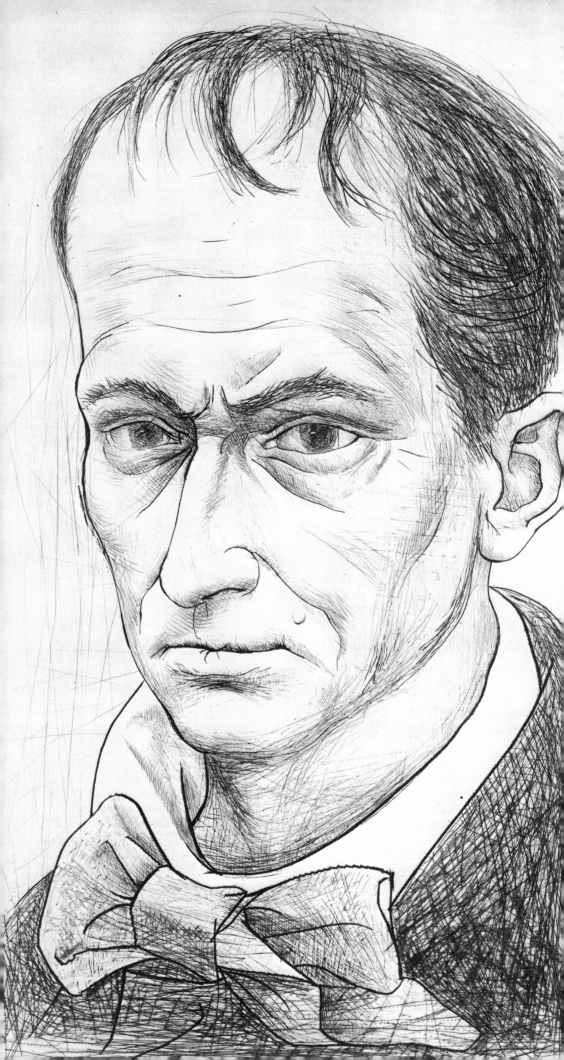

Ὸ ἘΑΥΙῸΝ
~~ΤΙΜΩ~~
ΤΙΜΩΡΟΎΜΕ
ΝΟΣ

L'HÉAYTONTIMOROYMÉNOS

Je suis la plaie et le couteau !
Je suis le soufflet et la joue !
Je suis les membres et la roue
Et la victime et le bourreau !

C. B.

A matchless sun, terrific, bright,
Deep in the vault of heaven was set,
And my poor eyeballs, burning yet,
Are blinded with excess of light.

In vain I strove, in vain presumed
To bend all Space to my desire,
I know not in what eye of fire
My wings are melted and consumed.

Like Icarus I hurtle down
And, scorched by Beauty's fatal flame,
I shall not even leave my name
Upon the sea in which I drown.

[JAMES LAVER]

CIV

Self-Communing

Be wise, my Sorrow, and be quiet too;
You called the Night, and lo, the Night is here;
And in the city, covered all from view,
She brings to some, sweet peace, to others, fear;
While the vile multitude, a grovelling crew,
Crouch 'neath the whip of pleasure, bought too dear,
And gather up remorse, their only due—
Give me your hand, my Sorrow; go not near!

Far from them, let us watch the vanished years,
In antique garb, on heaven's high battlement,
And sweet Regret, smiling amid her tears.
Under an arch the dead Sun falls asleep,
And in her long shroud, towards the Orient,
Listen, my love, and hear the soft night creep!

[JAMES LAVER]

CV

Heautontimoroumenos

I'll strike thee without enmity
Nor wrath,—like butchers at the block!
As Moses smote the living rock,
—Till from thine eyelids' agony

The springs of suffering shall flow
To slake the desert of my thirst;
And on that flood, my lust accurst
With Hope to fill its sails, shall go

As on the waves, a pitching barge,
And in my bosom quickening,
Thy sobs and tears I love shall ring
Loud as a drum that beats a charge!

For am I not a clashing note
In God's eternal symphony,
Thanks to this vulture, Irony,
Whose talons rend my heart and throat?

She's in my voice, the screaming elf!
My poisoned blood came all from her!
I am the mirror sinister
Wherein the vixen sees herself!

I am the wound and I the knife!
I am the blow I give, and feel!
I am the broken limbs, the wheel,
The hangman and the strangled life!

I am my heart's own vampire, for
I walk alone, condemned, forlorn,
By laughter everlasting torn,
Yet doomed to smile,—ah, nevermore!

[LEWIS PIAGET SHANKS]

CVI

The Irremediable

I

An Entity, an Eidolon,
Fallen from out some azure clime
Into a Styx of lead and slime
Nor star nor sun has looked upon;

A wandering angel indiscreet,
Lost in the love of things difform,
Who down abysmal dreams of harm
Falls beating as great swimmers beat,

And fights in mortal anguish stark
Some eddy of a demon sea
That sings and shouts deliriously
And dances in the whirling dark;

II

A hapless wretch ensorcelèd,
Who from a viper-swarming pit
In futile gropings infinite
Would reach the flown light overhead;

A lost soul without lamp descending,
To whom the gulf-arisen smell
Betrays a dank, profounder hell
And railless fall of stairs unending,

Where slimy monsters ward the way
Whose eyes of phosphor, luminous, large,
Make darker still the nighted marge—
Burning in bulks obscure for aye;

A vessel at the frozen pole
As in a trap of crystal caught,

And searching how her keel was brought
Thereto by fatal strait and shoal:—

Clear emblems, perfect similes
Of a fortune irremediable,
Showing the Devil is always able
To do the task that he decrees.

III

The heart, in sombre colloquy,
Mirrors itself in very sooth:
The dark and lucid well of Truth,
Where a star trembles lividly,

Flambeau of grace from sullen hells,
Pharos of ironies infernal,
Sole glory, solacement eternal—
Conscience in Evil ever dwells!

[CLARK ASHTON SMITH]

CVII

The Clock

Terrible Clock! God without mercy; mighty Power!
Saying all day, '*Remember!* Remember and beware:
There is no arrow of pain but in a tiny hour
Will make thy heart its target, and stick and vibrate there.

'Toward the horizon all too soon and out of sight
Vaporous Pleasure, like a sylphide, floats away;
Each instant swallows up one crumb of that delight
Accorded to each man for all his mortal day.'

The Second says, three thousand six hundred times
   an hour,
'*Remember!* Look, the wingèd insect Now doth sit
Upon thy vein, and shrilleth, "I am Nevermore,
And I have sucked thy blood; I am flying away with it!"

'*Remember! Souviens-toi! Esto memor!*—no tongue
My metal larynx does not speak—O frivolous man,
These minutes, rich in gold, slide past; thou art not young;
Remember! and wash well the gravel in the pan!

'*Remember!* Time, the player that need not cheat to win,
Makes a strong adversary. Is thy game begun?
Thy game is lost! Day wanes; night waxes. Look within
The gulf,—it still is thirsty. The sands are all but run.

'Soon, soon, the hour will strike, when Hazard, he
   that showed
A god-like face, when Virtue—thy bride, but still intact—
When even Repentance (oh, last inn along the road!)
Will say to thee, "Die, coward. It is too late to act." '

            [EDNA ST. VINCENT MILLAY]

Parisian Pictures

CVIII

A Landscape

I would, when I compose my solemn verse,
Sleep near the heaven as do astrologers,
Near the high bells, and with a dreaming mind
Hear their calm hymns blown to me on the wind.

Out of my tower, with chin upon my hands,
I'll watch the singing, babbling human bands;
And see clock-towers like spars against the sky,
And heavens that bring thoughts of eternity;

And softly, through the mist, will watch the birth
Of stars in heaven and lamplight on the earth;
The threads of smoke that rise above the town;
The moon that pours her pale enchantment down.

Seasons will pass till Autumn fades the rose;
And when comes Winter with his weary snows,
I'll shut the doors and window-casements tight,
And build my faery palace in the night.

Then I will dream of blue horizons deep;
Of gardens where the marble fountains weep;
Of kisses, and of ever-singing birds—
A sinless Idyll built of innocent words.

And Trouble, knocking at my window-pane
And at my closet door, shall knock in vain;
I will not heed him with his stealthy tread,
Nor from my reverie uplift my head;

For I will plunge deep in the pleasure still
Of summoning the spring-time with my will,
Drawing the sun out of my heart, and there
With burning thoughts making a summer air.

[JAMES HUNEKER]

CIX

The Sun

In this old district, where the shabby houses hide
Behind drawn shutters many a furtive lust inside,
In the fierce rays of noon, which mercilessly beat
On town and country, on the roofs and on the wheat,
I walk alone, absorbed in my fantastic play,—
Fencing with rhymes, which, parrying nimbly, back away;
Tripping on words, as on rough paving in the street,
Or bumping into verses I long had dreamed to meet.

The sun, our nourishing father, anaemia's deadly foe,
Makes poems, as if poems were roses, bud and grow;
Burns through the anxious mists of every mind alive,
And fills with honey the celled brain as the celled hive.
'Tis he who makes the man on crutches stump along
As gay as a young girl, humming as sweet a song;
Calls to the human spirit to climb and ripen still—
Which would bloom on for ever, could it have its will.

He goes into the city, where, like the poet, his light
Ennobles and gives purpose to the least thing in sight;
Or, quietly, unattended, like a king, he calls
At every palace, and visits all the hospitals.

[EDNA ST. VINCENT MILLAY]

CX

Lola de Valence

(INSCRIPTION FOR THE PICTURE BY ÉDOUARD MANET)

Friends, though on every side of you you see
Such beauties that desire must hesitate,
In Lola de Valence there scintillate
Strange charms o' a gem of rose and ebony.

[SIR JOHN SQUIRE]

CXI

The Offended Moon

O Moon, O lamp of hill and secret dale!
Thou whom our fathers, ages out of mind,
Worshipped in thy blue heaven, whilst behind
Thy stars streamed after thee a glittering trail,

Dost see the poet, weary-eyed and pale,
Or lovers on their happy beds reclined,
Showing white teeth in sleep, or vipers twined,
'Neath the dry sward; or in a golden veil

Stealest thou with faint footfall o'er the grass
As of old, to kiss from twilight unto dawn
The faded charms of thine Endymion? . . .

'O child of this sick century, I see
Thy grey-haired mother leering in her glass
And plastering the breast that suckled thee!'

[SIR JOHN SQUIRE]

CXII

To a Brown Beggar-Maid

White maiden with the russet hair,
Whose garments, through their holes, declare
That poverty is part of you,
And beauty too.

To me, a sorry bard and mean,
Your youthful beauty, frail and lean,
With summer freckles here and there,
Is sweet and fair.

Your sabots tread the roads of chance,
And not one queen of old romance
Carried her velvet shoes and lace
With half your grace.

In place of tatters far too short
Let the proud garments worn at Court
Fall down with rustling fold and pleat
About your feet;

In place of stockings, worn and old,
Let a keen dagger all of gold
Gleam in your garter for the eyes
Of roués wise;

Let ribbons carelessly untied
Reveal to us the radiant pride
Of your white bosom purer far
Than any star;

Let your white arms uncovered shine,
Polished and smooth and half divine;
And let your elfish fingers chase
With riotous grace

The purest pearls that softly glow,
The sweetest sonnets of Belleau,
Offered by gallants ere they fight
For your delight;

And many fawning rhymers who
Inscribe their first thin book to you
Will contemplate upon the stair
Your slipper fair;

And many a page who plays at cards,
And many lords and many bards,
Will watch your going forth, and burn
For your return;

And you will count before your glass
More kisses than the lily has;
And more than one Valois will sigh
When you pass by.

But meanwhile you are on the tramp,
Begging your living in the damp,
Wandering mean streets and alleys o'er,
From door to door;

And shilling bangles in a shop
Cause you with eager eyes to stop,
And I, alas, have not a sou
To give to you.

Then go, with no more ornament,
Pearl, diamond, or subtle scent,
Than your own fragile naked grace
And lovely face.

[F. P. STURM]

CXIII

The Swan

I

Andromache, I think of you!—This stream,
This Simoïs that now so mean appears
Once mirrored back your form, as in a dream,
Deep flowing, swollen with a widow's tears.

And as the new-built Carrousel I pass,
The curtains of my memory roll apart,
—Old Paris is no more (a town, alas!
Changes more quickly than the human heart).

And only in a dream I see this camp
Of workmen's huts, these bleached and broken bones
Of buildings, rotting on the pavements damp,
This bric-à-brac, bright shining on the stones.

There, in the former days, a circus stood,
And at that hour of morning, cold and wan,
When men go forth to labour, in the mud
Caked, and with garbage strewn, I saw a Swan.

A swan escaped, by hazard, from his cage,
That with his webbed feet trod the stony ground.
And in the gutter, with impuissant rage,
Sought for a trickle, but no water found.

To bathe in dust his draggled wing he tries,
Longs for his natal, well-remembered lake,
And moans, 'When peals the thunder in the skies?
When falls the rain my burning thirst to slake?'

And still towards the heavens, ironic, blue,
This strange, unhappy, fatal myth I see,
Like that poor banished man that Ovid drew,
Stretch his parched neck and curse his Deity.

II

Paris is changed in everything but name;
Gone tower and palace! In my heart alone
Nothing has moved, each symbol is the same.
My memories are heavier than stone.

And still hard by the Louvre, as in old time,
I think of my poor swan's wild agony,
Like wretched exiles, foolish and sublime,
Devoured by one desire; and then of thee,

Andromache, a hero's consort fair,
Now Pyrrhus' spoil, mere booty of men's strife,
Crouched o'er an empty tomb in wild despair,
Widow of Hector, and Helenus' wife.

I think of the poor Negress, doomed to die
Of hunger and disease, on every hand
Seeking with wild, uncomprehending eye
For the lost palm-trees of her native land.

I think of him who cannot find again
What he has lost, but through the endless hours,
Must suck from Sorrow's dugs the milk of pain,
And lost, starved children withering like flowers.

Thus, in the trackless forest of my mind,
An ancient Memory his trumpet blew.
I thought of castaways that none will find,
Of slaves, and vanquished . . . aye, and others, too.

[JAMES LAVER]

CXIV

The Seven Old Men

City swarming with people, how full you are of dreams!
Here in broad daylight, surely, the passer-by may meet
A spectre,—be accosted by him! Mystery seems
To move like a thick sap through every narrow street.

I thought (daybreak, it was, in a sad part of town)
'These houses look much higher in the fog!'—they stood
Like two grey quays between which a muddy stream
   flows down;
The setting of the play matched well the actor's mood.

All space became a dirty yellow fog; I tried
To fight it off; I railed at my poor soul, whose feet,
Weary already, dragged and stumbled at my side.
Big wagons, bound for market, began to shake the street.

Suddenly there beside me an old man—all in holes
His garments were, and yellow, like the murky skies,
A sight to wring a rain of coins from kindly souls,
Save for a certain malice gleaming in his eyes,—

Appeared. You would have said those eyeballs,
　　without doubt,
Were steeped in bile—they sharpened the sleet they
　　looked upon.
His beard, with its long hairs, stiff as a sword stood out
Before him, as the beard of Judas must have done.

He stooped so when he walked, his spine seemed
　　not so much
Bending as broken,—truly, his leg with his back-bone
Made a right angle; and his stick, the finishing touch,
Gave him the awkward gait—now rearing, now
　　half-thrown—

Of a three-legged Jew, or some lame quadruped.
It crossed my mind, as through the mud and snow he went,
'He walks like someone crushing the faces of the dead.
Hostile, that's what he is; he's not indifferent.'

A man exactly like him followed him. From beard
To stick they were the same, had risen from the same hell.
These centenarian twins kept step in rhythmic weird
Precision, toward some goal which doubtless they
　　knew well.

'What ugly game is this?' I said; 'what horseplay's here?
Am I the butt of knaves, or have I lost my mind?'
For seven times—I counted them—there did appear
This sinister form, which passed, yet left itself behind.

Let anyone who smiles at my distress, whose heart
No sympathetic horror grips, consider well:
Though these old monsters seemed about to fall apart,
Somehow I knew they were eternal,—I could tell!

Had I beheld one more of them, I think indeed
I should have died!—for each, in some disgusting way,
Had spawned himself, lewd Phoenix, from his own
    foul seed,
Was his own son and father,—I fled—I could not stay.

Angry, bewildered, like a drunken man by whom
All objects are seen double, I locked my door, and heard
My frozen heart cry out with dread in the hot room,—
That what was so mysterious should be so absurd!

My reason fought to gain the bridge and take the helm;
The tempest thrust it back; and rudderless, unrigged,
A hull which the waves wash but will not overwhelm,
My soul upon a shoreless sea of horror jigged.

[EDNA ST. VINCENT MILLAY]

CXV

The Little Old Women

I

Deep in the tortuous folds of ancient towns,
Where all, even horror, to enchantment turns,
I watch, obedient to my fatal mood,
For the decrepit, strange and charming beings,
The dislocated monsters that of old
Were lovely women—Laïs or Eponine!
Hunchbacked and broken, crooked though they be,
Let us still love them, for they still have souls.
They creep along wrapped in their chilly rags,
Beneath the whipping of the wicked wind,
They tremble when an omnibus rolls by,
And at their sides, a relic of the past,
A little flower-embroidered satchel hangs.

Lesbos, terre des nuits chaudes
                    et langoureuses,
Qui font qu'à leurs miroirs,
                    stérile volupté !
Les filles aux yeux creux,
                    De leurs corps amoureuses,
Caressent les fruits mûrs
                    De leur nubilité ;

Lesbos, terre
            des nuits chaudes
                    et langoureuses...

They trot about, most like to marionettes;
They drag themselves, as does a wounded beast;
Or dance unwillingly as a clapping bell
Where hangs and swings a demon without pity.
Though they be broken they have piercing eyes,
That shine like pools where water sleeps at night;
The astonished and divine eyes of a child
Who laughs at all that glitters in the world.
Have you not seen that most old women's shrouds
Are little, like the shroud of a dead child?
Wise Death, in token of his happy whim,
Wraps old and young in one enfolding sheet.
And when I see a phantom, frail and wan,
Traverse the swarming picture that is Paris,
It ever seems as though the delicate thing
Trod with soft steps towards a cradle new.
And then I wonder, seeing the twisted form,
How many times must workmen change the shape
Of boxes where at length such limbs are laid?
These eyes are wells brimmed with a million tears;
Crucibles where the cooling metal pales—
Mysterious eyes that are strong charms to him
Whose life-long nurse has been austere Disaster.

II

The love-sick vestal of the old 'Frascati';
Priestess of Thalia, alas! whose name
Only the prompter knows, and he is dead;
Bygone celebrities that in bygone days
The Tivoli o'ershadowed in their bloom;
All charm me; yet among these beings frail
Three, turning pain to honey-sweetness, said
To the Devotion that had lent them wings:
'Lift me, O powerful Hippogriffe, to the skies'—
One by her country to despair was driven;
One by her husband overwhelmed with grief;
One wounded by her child, Madonna-like;
Each could have made a river with her tears.

III

Oft have I followed one of these old women,
One among others, when the falling sun
Reddened the heavens with a crimson wound—
Pensive, apart, she rested on a bench
To hear the brazen music of the band,
Played by the soldiers in the public park
To pour some courage into citizens' hearts,
On golden eves when all the world revives.
Proud and erect she drank the music in,
The lively and the warlike call to arms;
Her eyes blinked like an ancient eagle's eyes;
Her forehead seemed to await the laurel crown!

IV

Thus you do wander, uncomplaining Stoics,
Through all the chaos of the living town:
Mothers with bleeding hearts, saints, courtesans,
Whose names of yore were on the lips of all;
Who were all glory and all grace, and now
None know you; and the brutish drunkard stops,
Insulting you with his derisive love;
And cowardly urchins call behind your back.
Ashamed of living, withered shadows all,
With fear-bowed backs you creep beside the walls,
And none salute you, destined to loneliness!
Refuse of Time ripe for Eternity!
But I, who watch you tenderly afar,
With unquiet eyes on your uncertain steps,
As though I were your father, I—O wonder!—
Unknown to you taste secret, hidden joy.
I see your maiden passions bud and bloom,
Sombre or luminous, and your lost days
Unroll before me while my heart enjoys
All your old vices, and my soul expands
To all the virtues that have once been yours.
Ruined! and my sisters! O congenerate hearts,
Octogenarian Eves o'er whom is stretched
God's awful claw, where will you be to-morrow?

[JAMES HUNEKER]

CXVI

The Blind

Consider them, my soul, how horrible!
Like draper's dummies vaguely ludicrous;
Singular as somnambulists; still thus
Rolling vain eyeballs, wherefore? who can tell?
Do pupils whence the spark divine has fled
Yet long to scan afar and, ill at ease,
Probe upward? Never o'er the pavement these
In pensive reverie droop the full-charged head.
They ford across an endless black abyss
That brother is to silence. Hear they this
City around them laugh and howl, and grind
At pleasure as at some atrocious task?
I too drag on, more stultified I ask:
What can we seek in Heaven, all we blind?

[T. STURGE MOORE]

CXVII

To a Passer-by

Around me thundered the deafening noise of the street,
In mourning apparel, portraying majestic distress,
With queenly fingers, just lifting the hem of her dress,
A stately woman passed by with hurrying feet.

Agile and noble, with limbs of perfect poise,
Ah, how I drank, thrilled through like a Being insane,
In her look, a dark sky, from whence springs forth
    the hurricane,
There lay but the sweetness that charms, and the joy
    that destroys.

A flash—then the night. . . . O loveliness fugitive!
Whose glance has so suddenly caused me again to live,
Shall I not see you again till this life is o'er?

Elsewhere, far away . . . too late, perhaps never more,
For I know not whither you fly, nor you, where I go,
O soul that I would have loved, and *that* you know!

[CYRIL SCOTT]

CXVIII

Skeletons Digging

I

Among the anatomical plates
Displayed along the dusty quays,
Where many a dead book desiccates
Like an old mummy—among these

Sad diagrams to which the grave
Fantasy and ironic skill
Of some forgotten artist have
Lent a mysterious beauty still,

One sees (for thus mere nerves and bones
Were rendered life-like through his pains)
Digging like labourers, skeletons
And skinless men composed of veins.

II

Out of that stony soil which ye
Unceasingly upturn, with all
The strength of your stripped vertebrae
And fleshless thews—funereal

Prisoners from the charnel pile!—
What do ye look for? Speak. What strange
Harvest prepare ye all this while?
What lord has bid you load his grange?

Do ye desire, O symbols clear
And frightful of a doom unguessed,
To demonstrate that even there,
In the deep grave, we have no rest—

That we can no more count as friend
Eternity than we can Time,
Death, too, being faithless in the end?
That we shall toil in dust and grime

For ever upon some field of shade,
And harry the stiff sod, and put
Over and over to the spade
A naked and ensanguined foot?

[GEORGE DILLON]

CXIX

Evening Twilight

Night falls, so welcome to the criminal;
Creeping it comes, like an accomplice;—all
The heavens slowly close their portals grey,
And restless man becomes a beast of prey.

O night, delicious night, long coveted
By men whose arms can say ere dusk is sped:
Truly we've worked to-day!—Night's shadowy hours
Solace the souls that cankering pain devours
—The self-willed scholar with his flagging brain,
The workman bent who seeks his bed again.

Meanwhile the evil demons of the air
Wake heavily, like men with many a care,
And flying, dash their heads on wall and blind.
Then, 'mid the gas-jets flickering in the wind,
—An ant-heap opening wide each gate and floor—
Pale Prostitution flames from every door;
Nowhere she does not clear a path, and crawl
As might an enemy who saps a wall;
A worm that steals the food poor men consume,
She wriggles through the mire and the gloom.
The kitchens sing around us everywhere,
Playhouses shriek and bands of music blare;
Each great hotel's another gambling-hall
Swarming with bawds and blacklegs, allies all,
While thieves, who truce nor mercy never knew,
Will presently begin their labours too,
And gently force the rich man's doors and gates
To buy a little food and clothe their mates.

Awake, my spirit, in this hour of fear,
And to its pandemonium close thy ear,
Now is the time when sick men's pains increase!
The murky Night is throttling them;—they cease
To live, and sink into the Gulf, undone.
Their groanings fill the poor-house.—More than one
Will seek no more, at dusk, his savoury bowl
Beside the hearth, near some beloved soul.

And most of them have never known the call
Of home, nor had a hearth, nor lived at all!

[LEWIS PIAGET SHANKS]

CXX

The Gaming-Table

On tarnished chairs the pale old harlots quiver,
Sly fatal eyes under the eyebrows painted
Dreadfully mincing: as their lean ears shiver
With hateful jewelled peal the air is tainted.

Round the green tables a frieze of lipless faces,
Of blue-cold lips, if lips, of toothless gums,
And fingers, fevered with Hell's last disgraces,
Fumbling in pockets—or in deliriums.

Dull chandeliers in the soot-mottled ceiling
And swollen lamps pick out with violet
Shadow the brows of famous poets, reeling
To waste the guerdon of art's blood-stained sweat.

My eye, turned inward, darkly can discern
This Hellish picture self-distorted thus,
The while I see in yonder taciturn
Corner myself, cold, mute—and envious.

Envying these creatures their tenacious lust,
These rattling skeletons their deadly mirth,
Envying all of those who gaily thrust
Honour or beauty to rot beneath the earth.

Envious my heart! O dark and dreadful word!
When these with passion their bright destruction bless,
Who drunk with the pulse of their own blood preferred
Deep pain to death and Hell to nothingness.

[HUMBERT WOLFE]

CXXI

Danse Macabre

Proud as a living woman of her height,
With gloves and handkerchief and great bouquet,
She flaunts her nonchalance and graces light,
And seems a slim coquette of yesterday.

Could any dancer show a slimmer waist?
Her ample robe, in royal splendour, flows
In folds about her dainty ankles, laced
In tufted pattens, lovely as a rose.

A frill of lace adorns her bony breast,
Like amorous rills amid the rocks at play,
And chastely shields from every silly jest
The charms of horror that it hides away.

Her eyes are wells of darkness, empty, wide;
Her skull, with flowers beautifully crowned,
Sways on her slender spine from side to side.
O spell of nothingness by Folly gowned!

Some, lovers of the flesh, perhaps would claim
Thou art a travesty. They do not know
The nameless beauty of the human frame.
Tall skeleton, my heart prefers thee so!

Dost come to trouble, with thy dreadful smile,
Life's festival? Or does some ancient fire
Still urge thy living carcass and beguile
Thee, fool, unto this Sabbath of Desire?

Dost hope, with violins and lights agleam,
To slay that mocking nightmare of unrest?
Art come to beg the orgy's rushing stream
To cool the hellfire kindled in thy breast?

Exhaustless fount of folly and of sin!
Alembic of our woe immutable!
I see the snake still wandering within
The trellis of thy ribs, insatiable.

But truth to tell, I fear thy coquetry
May find its efforts unrewarded long;
What mortal heart delights in raillery?
The charms of horror only thrill the strong!

Thine eyes, abyss where dreadful secrets lurk,
Breathe giddiness. No prudent cavaliers
Will view, nor vomit, the unchanging smirk
That on thy two and thirty teeth appears.

Yet who has not embraced a skeleton,
And fed on dreams of what the grave-worms eat?
What boots the perfume or the cloak we don?
Your scorn, fair critics, proves your own conceit.

O noseless dancer, whore we cannot flee,
Say to the partner who thy beauty shuns:
'Proud minions, 'neath your paint and powder, ye
All smell of death! O scented skeletons,

'Worn dandies, shaven fools with stinking breath,
Pale varnished corpses, grey decrepit beaux,
The world-wide rhythm of the Dance of Death
Is sweeping you to lands that no one knows!

'From Seine to Ganges hot, where'er you roam,
Death's herd is dancing, mad, incurious
Of the Dark Angel's trump that from the dome
Is thrust, an evil gaping blunderbuss.

'Death ogles thee both here and everywhere,
Writhing, ridiculous Humanity,
And oft, perfumed like thee, she comes to share
In irony, thine own insanity!'

[LEWIS PIAGET SHANKS]

CXXII

The Love of Lying

When I behold thee in thine indolence,
'Mid brazen notes that from the dome resound,
Trailing the graces of indifference
In rhythmic feet and weary gaze profound;

And when I view thy forehead, pale and wan,
So haunting in the gaslight's warm disguise,
Where evening's torches paint the rose of dawn,
Thine eyes that like a portrait's eyes entice,

I say: O rose bizarre, hast bloomed afresh!
For royal memories crown her, towering, vast,
And all her heart's a fruit, whose bruisèd flesh
Is, like her body, ripe for love at last.

Art thou October fruit of sovereign zest?
Art thou an urn for Sorrow's tearful hours,
A perfume wafting me to isles of rest,
A roseleaf bed or funeral wreath of flowers?

I know that there are eyes that seem to mourn,
Wherein no secret pearl of sorrow lies;
Fair empty caskets that no gems adorn,
As deep and bottomless as ye, O Skies!

But does it matter what thou really art,
O nectar in my soul, with truth at war?
What boots thy stupid or indifferent heart?
Hail, mask! It is thy beauty I adore.

[LEWIS PIAGET SHANKS]

CXXIII

Je n'ai pas oublié…

I have not forgotten the house I shared with you
In the suburbs, small and white, but quiet too.
A Venus and Pomona hid their bare
Worn stucco limbs in the scant shrubbery there;
And the sun at evening splendidly ablaze
Behind the panes that caught the glittering rays
As if he watched with open, curious eye
Our long and silent dinners from the sky,
Like candle-gleams his lavish glories shed
On the hanging serge, the frugal cloth we spread.

[SIR ERIC MACLAGAN]

CXXIV

La servante au grand cœur…

You were jealous of the maid, and her open love.
Now she is asleep, and the sods are bare above;
But we ought to take some flowers and leave them there.
The dead, the unhappy dead have much to bear.
When Autumn blows, and the old boughs are shed,
And the wind is drear on the grave-stones overhead,
Surely they think of the living asleep, and find
That some laid warm in bed are less than kind;
For gnawn by nightmares of the blackness, chill
Old skeletons where the worm has worked his will,
Robbed of kind talk, of nightly fellowship,
They feel the snows of winter soak and drip,
And the years pass, and friends and kindred fail;
For the wreaths rot unheeded from the rail.

When the damp log sings one evening, if I were
To find her sitting quietly in a chair,
Or on a blue cold night of wintry gloom
Come on her crouched in the corner of the room,
Risen grave and mother-like from under the mould
Of her last bed, to tend a child grown old,
What could I answer to a ghost so dear
Seeing her sunken eye, her trickling tear?

[SIR ERIC MACLAGAN]

CXXV

Mist and Rain

O muddy Aprils, autumns, winter days,
Seasons that lull to sleep! my love and praise
Are yours, for unto heart and brain ye bring
Your vaporous shrouds and tombs enveloping.

This boundless plain, where Boreas shrieks and plays,
This weather-vane, that nightly creaks and brays,
Arouse my soul far more than languorous spring,
And make it spread with joy its condor wing.

Dear months of mist that in the north prevail,
Naught is more sweet to souls that endless snows
Descend upon, and shadows grim enclose,

Than your unchanging twilight cold and pale,
—Unless some moonless eve should find us, twain,
Creeping in beds of chance to lull our pain.

[LEWIS PIAGET SHANKS]

CXXVI

Parisian Dream

I

That marvellous landscape of my dream—
Which no eye knows, nor ever will—
At moments, wide awake, I seem
To grasp, and it excites me still.

Sleep, how miraculous you are—
A strange caprice had urged my hand
To banish, as irregular,
All vegetation from that land;

And, proud of what my art had done,
I viewed my painting, knew the great
Intoxicating monotone
Of marble, water, steel and slate.

Staircases and arcades there were
In a long labyrinth, which led
To a vast palace; fountains there
Were gushing gold, and gushing lead.

And many a heavy cataract
Hung like a curtain,—did not fall,
As water does, but hung, compact,
Crystal, on many a metal wall.

Tall nymphs with Titan breasts and knees
Gazed at their images unblurred,
Where groves of colonnades, not trees,
Fringed a deep pool where nothing stirred.

Blue sheets of water, left and right,
Spread between quays of rose and green,
To the world's end and out of sight,
And still expanded, though unseen.

Enchanted rivers, those—with jade
And jasper were their banks bedecked;
Enormous mirrors, dazzled, made
Dizzy by all they did reflect.

And many a Ganges, taciturn
And heedless, in the vaulted air,
Poured out the treasure of its urn
Into a gulf of diamond there.

As architect, it tempted me
To tame the ocean at its source;
And this I did,—I made the sea
Under a jewelled culvert course.

And every colour, even black,
Became prismatic, polished, bright;
The liquid gave its glory back
Mounted in iridescent light.

There was no moon, there was no sun,—
For why should sun and moon conspire
To light such prodigies?—each one
Blazed with its own essential fire!

A silence like eternity
Prevailed, there was no sound to hear;
These marvels all were for the eye,
And there was nothing for the ear.

II

I woke; my mind was bright with flame;
I saw the cheap and sordid hole
I live in, and my cares all came
Burrowing back into my soul.

Brutally the twelve strokes of noon
Against my naked ear were hurled;
And a grey sky was drizzling down
Upon this sad, lethargic world.

[EDNA ST. VINCENT MILLAY]

CXXVII

Morning Twilight

The bugle-call across the barracks blared,
And in the wind of dawn the street-lamps flared.

It was the hour evil dreams are shed
On adolescents tossing in their bed;
When like a bleeding palpitating eye,
The lamp glows red against the livid sky;
When souls by cumbering bodies overborne
Struggle like candles with the gradual morn;
When through the air, a shivering army flees
Like tears on faces drying in the breeze,
And poets cease to write and maids to love.

Spirals of smoke arose, the roofs above.
Daughters of joy, wide-mouthed, with livid eye,
Lay sunk in stupid slumbers, all awry;
Or, dragging chill flat breasts across the bed,
Blew on their embers and their fingers red.
It was the hour when want and winter bring
More pain to women wrung by childbearing;
When, like a blood-choked, sobbing cry, afar,
A cock's crow rent the air crepuscular,
And seas of fog assailed the houses tall,
While dying men behind the poorhouse wall
Breathed their last broken gurgling sigh and died.
Exhausted rakes were riding home, outside.

Dawn, shivering in robes of pink and green,
Slowly advanced along the lonely Seine,
And dark-browed Paris, rubbing both his eyes,
Picked up his tools,—that toiler old and wise!

[LEWIS PIAGET SHANKS]

Wine

CXXVIII

The Soul of Wine

One eve in the bottle sang the soul of wine:
'Man, unto thee, dear disinherited,
I sing a song of love and light divine—
Prisoned in glass beneath my seals of red.

'I know thou labourest on the hill of fire,
In sweat and pain beneath a flaming sun,
To give the life and soul my vines desire,
And I am grateful for thy labours done.

'For I find joys unnumbered when I lave
The throat of man by travail long outworn,
And his hot bosom is a sweeter grave
Of sounder sleep than my cold caves forlorn.

'Hearest thou not the echoing Sabbath sound?
The hope that whispers in my trembling breast?
Thy elbows on the table! gaze around;
Glorify me with joy and be at rest.

'To thy wife's eyes I'll bring their long-lost gleam,
I'll bring back to thy child his strength and light,
To him, life's fragile athlete I will seem
Rare oil that firms his muscles for the fight.

'I flow in man's heart as ambrosia flows;
The grain the eternal Sower casts in the sod—
From our first loves the first fair verse arose,
Flower-like aspiring to the heavens and God!'

[JAMES HUNEKER]

CXXIX

The Scavenger's Bottle

Many a time by some reflected lamp,
Whose flickering flame is tortured by the wind,
Afar in some deep alley—loathsome, damp,
With its fermenting mass of human kind—

We see a scavenger go staggering by,
Clutching at nothing as a poet might,
Careless of all the crowd's cruel mockery,
Pour out his heart in dreams and projects bright;

Breathe solemn vows, and dictate laws supreme,
Endow the pauper, shelter the opprest,
Then glow with all the regal powers that seem
To have their very centre in his breast.

Struggling with woes unutterably deep,
Shivering with famine, and with age worn down,
Reeling and tottering 'neath the mighty heap
Of all the outcast refuse of the town.

These very people, smelling of the lees
Of wine butts, pass again with comrades grey
With battles fought on distant lands and seas—
Flags and triumphal arches o'er their way

Unfold before them, magic splendours rise,
And with the sunbeams dazzling from above,
With drums and braying clarions and loud cries,
They bring back glory to a people drunk with love.

Changing Pactolus-like its banks to gold,
Wine rolls across Humanity's drear plain,
Singing, thro' mortal throats, its exploits bold,
And reigning by its gifts, as monarchs reign.

To lull the pain—to still the rancour deep
Of these old wretches who in silence fall,
God, half-remorseful, had created sleep.
Man added wine, the sweetest gift of all.

[HARRY CURWEN]

CXXX

The Murderer's Wine

My wife is dead and I am free,
Now I may drink to my content;
When I came back without a cent
Her piteous outcries tortured me.

Now I am happy as a king,
The air is pure, the sky is clear;
Just such a summer as that year,
When first I went a-sweethearting.

A horrible thirst is tearing me,
To quench it I should have to swill
Just as much cool wine as would fill
Her tomb—that's no small quantity.

I threw her down and then began
To pile upon her where she fell
All the great stones around the well—
I shall forget it if I can.

By all the soft vows of our prime,
By those eternal oaths we swore,
And that our love might be once more
As 'twas in our old passionate time,

I begged her in a lonely spot
To come and meet me at nightfall;
She came, mad creature—we are all
More or less crazy, are we not?

She was quite pretty still, my wife,
Though she was very tired, and I,
I loved her too much, that is why
I said to her, 'Come, quit this life.'

No one can grasp my thought aright;
Did any of these sodden swine
Ever conceive a shroud of wine
On his most strangely morbid night?

Dull and insensible above
Iron machines, that stupid crew,
Summer or winter, never knew
The agonies of real love.

So now I am without a care!
Dead-drunk this evening I shall be,
Then fearlessly, remorselessly
Shall lie out in the open air

And sleep there like a homeless cur;
Some cart may rumble with a load
Of stones or mud along the road
And crush my head—I shall not stir.

Some heavy dray incontinent
May come and cut me clean in two:
I laugh at thought o't as I do
At Devil, God, and Sacrament.

[SIR JOHN SQUIRE]

CXXXI

The Solitary's Flagon

The luring glances of a hussy fair
Who glides toward you like the silver wake
Of sinuous moonlight on the trembling lake,
When Phoebe bathes her charms unconscious there,

The gambler's last resounding sack of gold,
The wanton kiss of love-worn Adeline,
The trailing melodies whose notes enshrine
Dim strains of human sorrows unconsoled,

All these, O bottle deep, were never worth
The pungent balsams in thine ample girth
Held for the pious poet's thirsty heart;

Thou givest hope and youth and strength anew,
—And pride, so dear to all the beggar-crew,
That sets us like triumphant gods, apart!

[LEWIS PIAGET SHANKS]

CXXXII

The Wine of Lovers

Space rolls to-day her splendour round!
Unbridled, spurless, without bound,
Mount we upon the wings of wine
For skies fantastic and divine!

Let us, like angels tortured by
Some wild delirious phantasy,
Follow the far-off mirage born
In the blue crystal of the morn.

And gently balanced on the wing
Of the wild whirlwind we will ride,
Rejoicing with the joyous thing.

My sister, floating side by side,
Fly we unceasing whither gleams
The distant heaven of my dreams.

[JAMES HUNEKER]

Flowers of Evil

CXXXIII

Dedication for a Banned Book

Reader puritanical,
If this book of mine you see,
Cast it from you hastily;
Gloomy 'tis, and full of gall,

Unless you've heard the Master's call,
Unless you've taken your degree
In Satan's University,
You will not understand at all.

But if, not fearing vertigo,
Your eye the dizzy height endures,
Read me, and learn to love me too;

And pity me, a soul like yours,
A soul in search of Paradise—
Or else my curse upon you lies!

[JAMES LAVER]

CXXXIV

Sin

For me the most foul demon still doth plot;
About me like the imponderable air
He flows. I drink him, and straightway am hot
With shameful lusts the tongue may not declare.
And since he knows how I love form, he wins
My soul in woman's guise, or else he'll tell
Some pious tale of washing out my sins
To tempt me to a draught that's brewed in Hell.

« ... Pour un de ces regards charmant,
  Baume divin,

  Des plaisirs plus obscurs
  je lèverai les voiles

  Et je t'endormirai
  dans un rêve
  Sans fin ! »

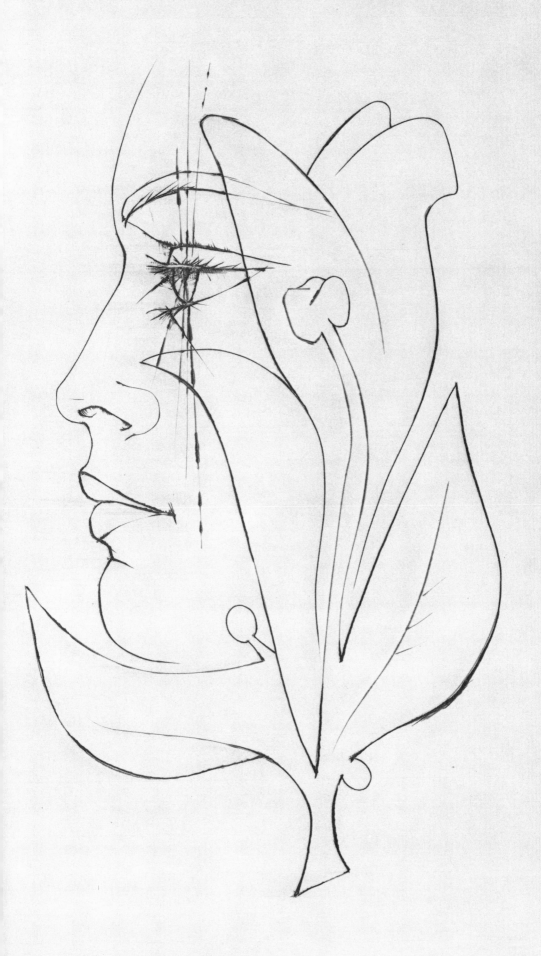

He leads me far away from God's clear eyes,
Halt and most sore still am I onward lured
To endless plains of speechless miseries,
Whereon unto my weary eyes and blurred
He shows red scars, foul raiment, and the shape
Of gory Ruin with her wounds a-gape.

[WILFRID THORLEY]

CXXXV

Murdered Woman
(DRAWING OF AN UNKNOWN MASTER)

Flasks of expensive scent, embroideries, rich brocades,
Taffeta sofas, satin chairs;
Statues in marble, paintings; fragrance that pervades
The empty, sumptuous gowns; warm airs

And sweet,—yet sultry, damp, unhealthful to inhale:
That sickening green-house atmosphere
Dying bouquets in their glass coffins give—a stale
Voluptuous chamber . . . Lying here

A corpse without a head, whence flows in a bright stream,
Making an ever broadening stain,
The red and living blood, which the white pillows seem
To lap up like a thirsty plain.

Pale as those awful shapes that out of shadow stare,
Chaining our helpless eyes to theirs,
The head, with its great mass of rich and sombre hair—
The ear-rings still in the small ears—

Like a ranunculus on the night-table sits;
And, void of thought, blank as the light
Of dawn, a glinting vague regard escapes from its
Eyeballs, up-rolled and china-white.

The headless trunk, in shameless posture on the bed,
Naked, in loose abandon lies,
Its secret parts exposed, its treasures all outspread
As if to charm a lover's eyes.

One sequined stocking, pink against the milky thigh,
Remains, pathetic souvenir;
The jewelled garter, like a flashing, secret eye,
Darts and withdraws a diamond leer.

A languorous portrait on the wall contrives to give
Force to the singular effect
Of the deep solitude,—the eyes provocative,
The pose inviting, half-erect.

The ghost of something strange and guilty, of some feast
Involving most improper fare,
Demoniac kisses, all obscure desires released,
Swims in the silent curtains there.

And yet, that fragile shoulder, that fine hand and arm—
How delicate the curve they make!—
The pelvic bones so sweetly pointed, the whole form
Lithe as a teased and fighting snake!—

She must have been quite young . . . her senses, all her soul,
Avid for life and driven wild
By tedium, set ajar, it may be, to the whole
Pack of perversions . . . ah, poor child!

Did he at length, that man, his awful thirst too great
For living flesh to satisfy,
On this inert, obedient body consummate
His lust?—O ravished corpse, reply!

Answer me, impure thing! Speak, frightening head,
    and tell:
Lifting you up by your long hair,
Did he on your cold teeth imprint in last farewell
One kiss, before he set you there?

Far from the mocking world, the peering crowd, oh far
From inquest, coroner, magistrate,
Sleep; sleep in peace; I leave you lying as you are,
Mysterious unfortunate.

In vain your lover roves the world; the thought of you
Troubles each chamber where he lies:
Even as you are true to him, he will be true
To you, no doubt, until he dies.

[EDNA ST. VINCENT MILLAY]

CXXXVI

Women Accurst

Like brooding cattle crouched along the sands
To the sea's utmost verge they turn their eyes,
And their feet mingle, and their groping hands
Learn bitter shudderings, languid ecstasies.

Some, whom unending confidences please,
Spell out their tales of timid girlish love,
And score the green bark of the sapling trees
Where the brook babbles through the hidden grove;

Others, a solemn sisterhood they seem,
Through spectre-haunted crags are moving slow,
Where naked breasts rose like a lava stream
And flushed for tempted Anthony long ago.

These, where the flaring torches drip with gum
In some old pagan cavern, hushed and deep,
Bid Bacchus heal their fevered moans, and come
To lull the memories of remorse to sleep.

And these, whose bosoms crave the scapular,
Who hide a scourge beneath the gowns they train,
Mix in lone nights, in shadowy woods afar,
The froth of pleasure with the tears of pain.

Ah virgins, demons, monsters, martyr host,
High souls, that dare reality despise,
Saints, satyrs, pilgrims for the infinite coast,
Now prodigal of tears, and now of cries,

Poor sisters, all my pity and love are yours
Whom to that hell my spirit has pursued,
For the dull pain, the thirst that still endures,
The tide of passion in your hearts renewed.

[SIR ERIC MACLAGAN]

CXXXVII

The Two Good Sisters

Debauch and Death are two detestable Hags,
Rich and ribald and of kisses prodigal,
Whose virginal wombs are always draped in rags,
Whose fervent ardours are demi-virginal.

To the Sinister Poet, enemy of men's money-bags,
Favourite of Hell, Courtesan and Cardinal,
Tombs and brothels show under the infernal flags
A bed remorse frequented never, maniacal.

And the coffin and the alcove pregnant to bestir me
Offer to all of us, like two sisters, listless leisures,
Fearful sweetnesses and intolerable pleasures.

Debauch, with unclean arms, when will you enter me?
O Death, when will you, her rival, her wiles being quaffed,
On her black cypresses your infected myrtles ingraft?

[ARTHUR SYMONS]

CXXXVIII

The Fountain of Blood

It seems to me sometimes my blood is bubbling out
As fountains do, in rhythmic sobs; I feel it spout
And lapse; I hear it plainly; it makes a murmuring sound;
But from what wound it wells, so far I have not found.

As blood runs in the lists, round tumbled armoured bones,
It soaks the city, islanding the paving-stones;
Everything thirsty leans to lap it, with stretched head;
Trees suck it up; it stains their trunks and branches red.

I turn to wine for respite, I drink, and I drink deep;
(Just for one day, one day, neither to see nor hear!)
Wine only renders sharper the frantic eye and ear.

In terror I cry to love, 'Oh, put my mind to sleep!'
But love for me is only a mattress where I shrink
On needles, and my blood is given to whores to drink.

[EDNA ST. VINCENT MILLAY]

CXXXIX

An Allegory

Here is a woman, richly clad and fair,
Who in her wine dips her long, heavy hair;
Love's claws, and that sharp poison which is sin,
Are dulled against the granite of her skin.
Death she defies, Debauch she smiles upon,
For their sharp scythe-like talons every one
Pass by her in their all-destructive play;
Leaving her beauty till a later day.
Goddess she walks; sultana in her leisure;
She has Mohammed's faith that heaven is pleasure,
And bids all men forget the world's alarms

Upon her breast, between her open arms.
She knows, and she believes, this sterile maid,
Without whom the world's onward dream would fade,
That bodily beauty is the supreme gift
Which may from every sin the terror lift.
Hell she ignores, and Purgatory defies;
And when black Night shall roll before her eyes,
She will look straight in Death's grim face forlorn,
Without remorse or hate—as one new born.

[JAMES HUNEKER]

CXL

Beatrice

In a burnt, ashen land, where no herb grew,
I to the winds my cries of anguish threw;
And in my thoughts, in that sad place apart,
Pricked gently with the poignard o'er my heart.
Then in full noon above my head a cloud
Descended tempest-swollen, and a crowd
Of wild, lascivious spirits huddled there,
The cruel and curious demons of the air,
Who coldly to consider me began;
Then, as a crowd jeers some unhappy man,
Exchanging gestures, winking with their eyes—
I heard a laughing and a whispering rise:

'Let us at leisure contemplate this clown,
This shadow of Hamlet aping Hamlet's frown,
With wandering eyes and hair upon the wind.
Is't not a pity that this empty mind,
This tramp, this actor out of work, this droll,
Because he knows how to assume a rôle
Should dream that eagles and insects, streams and woods,
Stand still to hear him chaunt his dolorous moods?
Even unto us, who made these ancient things,
The fool his public lamentation sings.'

With pride as lofty as the towering cloud,
I would have stilled these clamouring demons loud,
And turned in scorn my sovereign head away
Had I not seen—O sight to dim the day!—
There in the middle of the troupe obscene
The proud and peerless beauty of my Queen!
She laughed with them at all my dark distress,
And gave to each in turn a vile caress.

[JAMES HUNEKER]

CXLI

A Voyage to Cythera

My heart was like a bird and took to flight,
Around the rigging circling joyously;
The ship rolled on beneath a cloudless sky
Like a great angel drunken with the light.

'What is yon isle, sad and funereal?'
'Cythera, famed in deathless song,' say they,
'The gay old bachelors' Eldorado—Nay,
Look! 'tis a poor bare country after all!'

Isle of sweet secrets and heart banquetings!
The queenly shade of antique Venus thrills
Scentlike above thy level seas and fills
Our souls with languor and all amorous things.

Fair island of green myrtles and blown flowers
Held holy by all men for evermore,
Where the faint sighs of spirits that adore
Float like rose-incense through the quiet hours,

And dovelike sounds each murmured orison:—
Cythera lay there barren 'neath bright skies,
A rocky waste rent by discordant cries:
Natheless I saw a curious thing thereon.

No shady temple was it, close enshrined
I' the trees; no flower-crowned priestess hither came
With her young body burnt by secret flame,
Baring her breast to the caressing wind;

But when so close to the land's edge we drew
Our canvas scared the sea-fowl—gradually
We knew it for a three-branched gallows tree
Like a black cypress stark against the blue.

A rotten carcase hung, whereon did sit
A swarm of foul black birds; with writhe and shriek
Each sought to pierce and plunge his knife-like beak
Deep in the bleeding trunk and limbs of it.

The eyes were holes; the belly opened wide,
Streaming its heavy entrails on the thighs;
The grim birds, gorged with dreadful delicacies,
Had dug and furrowed it on every side.

Beneath the blackened feet there strove and pressed
A herd of jealous beasts with upward snout,
And in the midst of these there turned about
One, the chief hangman, larger than the rest . . .

Lone Cytherean! now all silently
Thou sufferest these insults to atone
For those old infamous sins that thou hast known,
The sins that locked the gate o' the grave to thee.

Mine are thy sorrows, ludicrous corse; yea, all
Are mine! I stood thy swaying limbs beneath,
And, like a bitter vomit, to my teeth
There rose old sorrows in a stream of gall.

O thou unhappy devil, I felt afresh,
Gazing at thee, the beaks and jaws of those
Black savage panthers and those ruthless crows,
Who loved of old to macerate my flesh.

The sea was calm, the sky without a cloud;
Henceforth for me all things that came to pass
Were blood and darkness,—round my heart, alas!
There clung that allegory, like a shroud.

Naught save mine image on a gibbet thrust
Found I on Venus' island desolate . . . .
Ah, God! the courage and strength to contemplate
My body and my heart without disgust!

[SIR JOHN SQUIRE]

CXLII

Cupid and the Skull
(OLD ENGRAVING)

Love, in his sacrilegious pride,
Of laughter full,
As on a throne he sits astride
The human skull,

Blows his gay bubbles in the air;
They float up high,
As if to join the planets where
They touch the sky.

These luminous and fragile balls
Gigantic seem,
And then, in turn, each bursts and falls,
Gone like a dream.

And, as each bursts, I hear a cry,
Half-prayer, half-groan:
'Oh, when shall this game cease, and I
Be left alone?

'For what you use in sportive mood
So heedlessly,
Ah, cruel! is the flesh, and blood
And heart of me!'

[JAMES LAVER]

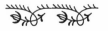

Revolt

CXLIII

The Denial of Peter

What does God care for the fierce curse and cry
Which mounts all day to His dear Seraphim?
A glutton and a wine swiller, to Him
Our acid blasphemies sing lullaby.

Sobs of the martyred and the crucified
Make fascinating music, as it seems;
Although blood gushes out for it in streams!
The heaven's lust is never satisfied.

—Jesus! remember, you grovelled to repeat
Prayers in the bitter garden, sweated blood
For One who in His heaven laughed aloud
To hear the nails tear through your hands and feet.

When your divinity was spat upon
By offal from the streets and bodyguard
And when you felt the sharp thorns driven hard
Into your skull, where love for man lived on,

When the dead weight of body, crushed by shock,
Pulled your arms from their sockets, and the red
Blood ran with sweat, disfiguring your head,
When you were placarded for all to mock,

Did you remember those bright sunny hours
When you fulfilled the promises of God,
When, mounted on a gentle ass, you trod
Roads paved and hung with palm-leaves and with flowers,

When, confident in courage, hope and pride
You drove the money changers out by force
And were indeed the Master? Did remorse,
Before the spear, not penetrate your side?

—I turn away, find more acceptable
A world where dreams need not be action's lord.
Take up the sword and perish by the sword?
Saint Peter denies Christ—he has done well!

[A. GRAHAM REYNOLDS]

CXLIV

Cain and Abel

Race of Abel, drink and be sleeping:
God shall smile on thee from the sky.

Race of Cain, in thy filth be creeping
Where no seeds of the serpents die.

Race of Abel, thy sacrifices
Shall flatter the nose of the Seraphim;

Race of Cain, shall thy devil's devices
Come to an end in any Inn?

Race of Abel, time for thy seed-time
And for thy cattle to be accursed.

Race of Cain, shall there not bleed time
In thine entrails that howl with thirst?

Race of Abel, warm thy belly in caverns
When the midnight hour is stark.

Race of Cain, tremble in thy taverns
As thou hearest the jackals bark.

Race of Abel, fear not pollution!
God begets the children of nights.

Race of Cain, in thy heart's solution
Extinguish thy cruel appetites.

Race of Abel, drowse and be trembling
As the lice in the haunted wood!

Race of Cain, on the roads dissembling
Trail thy progeny that cries for blood!

Ah, race of Abel, thy carrion's bloody
And shall follow the smoking soil!

Race of Cain, thy head that's muddy
Is not made for the viper's coil.

Race of Abel, let thy shame be shriven:
The sword is vanquished by the rod!

Race of Cain, mount up to thy heaven
And cast from heaven to the earth thy God!

[ARTHUR SYMONS]

CXLV

Litany to Satan

O grandest of the Angels, and most wise,
O fallen God, fate-driven from the skies,
Satan, at last take pity on our pain.

O first of exiles who endurest wrong,
Yet growest, in thy hatred, still more strong,
Satan, at last take pity on our pain.

O subterranean King, omniscient,
Healer of man's immortal discontent,
Satan, at last take pity on our pain.

To lepers and to outcasts thou dost show
That Passion is the Paradise below.
Satan, at last take pity on our pain.

Thou by thy mistress Death hast given to man
Hope, the imperishable courtesan.
Satan, at last take pity on our pain.

Thou givest to the Guilty their calm mien
Which damns the crowd around the guillotine.
Satan, at last take pity on our pain.

Thou knowest the corners of the jealous Earth
Where God has hidden jewels of great worth.
Satan, at last take pity on our pain.

Thou dost discover by mysterious signs
Where sleep the buried people of the mines.
Satan, at last take pity on our pain.

Thou stretchest forth a saving hand to keep
Such men as roam upon the roofs in sleep.
Satan, at last take pity on our pain.

Thy power can make the halting Drunkard's feet
Avoid the peril of the surging street.
Satan, at last take pity on our pain.

Thou, to console our helplessness, didst plot
The cunning use of powder and of shot.
Satan, at last take pity on our pain.

Thy awful name is written as with pitch
On the unrelenting foreheads of the rich.
Satan, at last take pity on our pain.

In strange and hidden places thou dost move
Where women cry for torture in their love.
Satan, at last take pity on our pain.

Father of those whom God's tempestuous ire
Has flung from Paradise with sword and fire,
Satan, at last take pity on our pain.

PRAYER

Satan, to thee be praise upon the Height
Where thou wast king of old, and in the night
Of Hell, where thou dost dream on silently.
Grant that one day beneath the Knowledge-tree,
When it shoots forth to grace thy royal brow,
My soul may sit, that cries upon thee now.

[JAMES ELROY FLECKER]

Death

CXLVI

The Death of Lovers

We shall have beds perfumed with sweet bouquet,
Sink in divans as utter as the tomb,
And blossoms blown in some strange, lovelier day
Will deck for us the ledges of our room.

Then, as the final heats consume away
From our contending hearts, they will illume
Like two vast torches, and reflect their ray
In the twin mirrors which our souls become.

Until one evening, rosy, mystic blue,
A sudden flash will shake our bodies through
Like a long sob, charged with the last farewell.

Long afterwards an angel will return
Through doors ajar, and joyfully dispel
The mirrors' tarnish, make the dead flames burn.

[A. GRAHAM REYNOLDS]

CXLVII

The Death of the Poor

Death is our sustenance, and makes us seize
Hold on our life: it is the end, the high
Hope that is like a cordial we buy
And till the evening strengthens our weak knees;

Beyond the snows, the frosts, the storms that freeze,
The tremor of a light beneath a sky
Of visible darkness, and the hostelry
Where we may eat and sleep and take our ease.

It is an angel, in whose quickening palms
Are folded joyous dreams and slumberous calms,
Who makes the bed of naked men and poor;

It is of God the mystic granary,
The long home of the homeless, and his store;
The door that opens on the unfathomed sky.

[MARGARET JOURDAIN]

CXLVIII

The Death of the Artists

How many times must I shake my stupid shins
Before I kiss your hideous visage, Caricature?
To hit the mark, O mystical quadrature,
How many, O quiver, lose of my javelins?

We lose our soul in subtle plots to save our sins,
We must demolish many a sinister Signature
Before we seize the great Creature's nomenclature,
Whose infernal desire throbs in our sensitive skins!

There are those who have never known their Idol,
And these damned Sculptors, and their Capuchins
Who at the Confessional absolve our sins,
Have but one hope, O Paris, for some Bridal!

And as the whirling world before us spins
Let Death rush to the abyss fast in Hell's gins!

[ARTHUR SYMONS]

CXLIX

The Day's End

Under wan and hueless light
Life, that knows not rest nor shame,
Runs or writhes without an aim;
So, when on the verge of sight

Rises the voluptuous Night,
Making even hunger stay,
Hiding even shame away,
Saith the poet, 'O delight!

'Rest at length for limbs and mind!
With a weary heart that holds
Nought but visions gloomiest,

'Now I will lie down to rest,
Wrapped within your curtained folds,
Darkness comforting and kind!'

[ARTHUR REED ROPES]

CL

A Dream of Death

Thinkest thou then, as I do, that thou art
Alone this mingled pain and joy to find?
—I was about to die, and in my heart
Desire and horror strangely intertwined.

Anguish and hope had each an equal part,
(The sands were running out) and in my mind
I felt pain's bliss and pleasure's bitter smart,
And the familiar world was left behind.

And like a child at its first pantomime,
After what seemed interminable time,
I knew the truth I only guessed before.

Death held no mystery; 'twas grey and chill
As dawn. I cried: 'What, is there nothing more?
The curtain's risen, and I am waiting still.'

[JAMES LAVER]

CLI

The Voyage

I

The world is equal to the child's desire
Who plays with pictures by his nursery fire—
How vast the world by lamplight seems! How small
When memory's eyes look back, remembering all!—

One morning we set forth with thoughts aflame,
Or heart o'erladen with desire or shame;
And cradle, to the song of surge and breeze,
Our own infinity on the finite seas.

Some flee the memory of their childhood's home;
And others flee their fatherland; and some,
Star-gazers drowned within a woman's eyes,
Flee from the tyrant Circe's witcheries;

And, lest they still be changed to beasts, take flight
For the embrasured heavens, and space, and light,
Till one by one the stains her kisses made
In biting cold and burning sunlight fade.

But the true voyagers are they who part
From all they love because a wandering heart

Drives them to fly the Fate they cannot fly;
Whose call is ever 'On!'—they know not why.

Their thoughts are like the clouds that veil a star;
They dream of change as warriors dream of war;
And strange wild wishes never twice the same:
Desires no mortal man can give a name.

II

We are like whirling tops and rolling balls—
For even when the sleepy night-time falls,
Old Curiosity still thrusts us on,
Like the cruel Angel who goads forth the sun.

The end of fate fades ever through the air,
And, being nowhere, may be anywhere
Where a man runs, hope waking in his breast,
For ever like a madman, seeking rest.

Our souls are wandering ships outwearièd;
And one upon the bridge asks: 'What's ahead?'
The topman's voice with an exultant sound
Cries: 'Love and Glory!'—then we run aground.

Each isle the pilot signals when 'tis late,
Is El Dorado, promised us by fate—
Imagination, spite of her belief,
Finds, in the light of dawn, a barren reef.

Oh the poor seeker after lands that flee!
Shall we not bind and cast into the sea
This drunken sailor whose ecstatic mood
Makes bitterer still the water's weary flood?

Such is an old tramp wandering in the mire,
Dreaming the paradise of his own desire,
Discovering cities of enchanted sleep
Where'er the light shines on a rubbish heap.

Celui qui veut unir dans
un accord mystique
L'ombre avec la chaleur,
la nuit avec le jour,
Ne chauffera Jamais son corps
paralytique
À ce rouge soleil
qu'on nomme
l'amour !

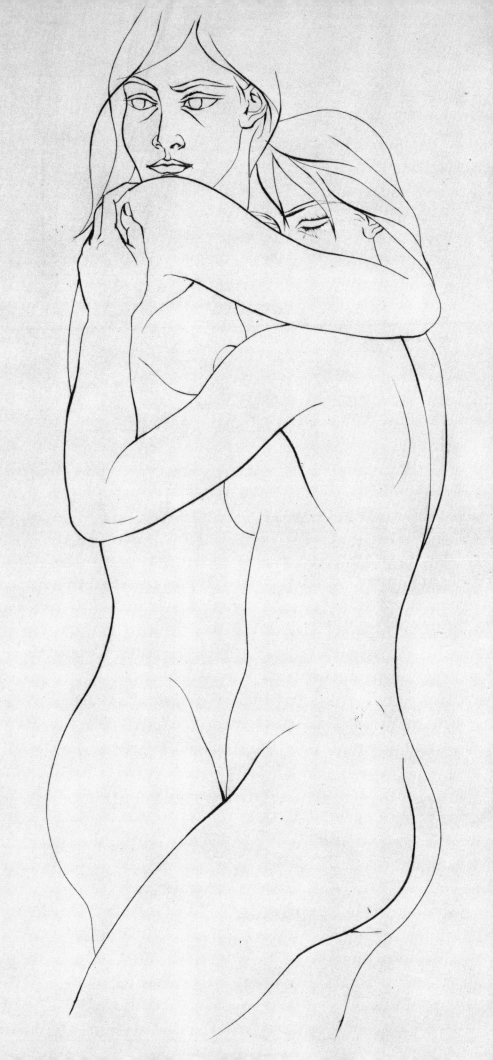

III

Strange voyagers, what tales of noble deeds
Deep in your dim sea-weary eyes one reads!
Open the casket where your memories are,
And show each jewel, fashioned from a star;

For I would travel without sail or wind,
And so, to lift the sorrow from my mind,
Let your long memories of sea-days far fled
Pass o'er my spirit like a sail outspread.

What have you seen?

IV

                    'We have seen waves and stars,
And lost sea-beaches, and known many wars,
And notwithstanding war and hope and fear,
We were as weary there as we are here.

'The lights that on the violet sea poured down,
The suns that set behind some far-off town,
Lit in our hearts the unquiet wish to fly
Deep in the glimmering distance of the sky;

'The loveliest countries that rich cities bless,
Never contained the strange wild loveliness
By fate and chance shaped from the floating cloud—
And we were always sorrowful and proud!

'Desire from joy gains strength in weightier measure.
Desire, old tree who draw'st thy sap from pleasure,
Though thy bark thicken as the years pass by,
Thine arduous branches rise towards the sky;

'And wilt thou still grow taller, tree more fair
Than the tall cypress?
                    —There have we, with care,
Gathered some flowers to please your eager mood,
Brothers who dream that distant things are good!

'We have seen many a jewel-glimmering throne;
And bowed to Idols when wild horns were blown
In palaces whose faery pomp and gleam
To your rich men would be a ruinous dream;

'And robes that were a madness to the eyes;
Women whose teeth and nails were stained with dyes;
Wise jugglers round whose neck the serpent winds—'

V

And then, and then what more?

VI

'O childish minds!

'Forget not that which we found everywhere,
From top to bottom of the fatal stair,
Above, beneath, around us and within,
The weary pageant of immortal sin.

'We have seen woman, stupid slave and proud,
Before her own frail, foolish beauty bowed;
And man, a greedy, cruel, lascivious fool,
Slave of the slave, a ripple in a pool;

'The martyrs' groan, the headsman's merry mood;
And banquets seasoned and perfumed with blood;
Poison, that gives the tyrant's power the slip;
And nations amorous of the brutal whip;

'Many religions not unlike our own,
All in full flight for heaven's resplendent throne;
And Sanctity, seeking delight in pain,
Like a sick man of his own sickness vain;

'And mad mortality, drunk with its own power,
As foolish now as in a bygone hour,
Shouting, in presence of the tortured Christ:
"I curse thee, mine own Image sacrificed."

'And those less mad, yet loving Lunacy,
Fleeing the troops herded by destiny,
Who seek for peace in opiate slumber furled—
Such is the pageant of the rolling world!'

VII

O bitter knowledge that the wanderers gain!
The world says our own age is little and vain;
For ever, yesterday, to-day, to-morrow,
'Tis horror's oasis in the sands of sorrow.

Must we depart? If you can rest, remain;
Part, if you must. Some fly, some cower in vain,
Hoping that Time, the grim and eager foe,
Will pass them by; and some run to and fro

Like the Apostles or the Wandering Jew;
Go where they will, the Slayer goes there too!
And there are some, and these are of the wise,
Who die as soon as birth has lit their eyes.

But when at length the Slayer treads us low,
We will have hope and cry, ' 'Tis time to go!'
As when of old we parted for Cathay
With wind-blown hair and eyes upon the bay.

We will embark upon the Shadowy Sea,
Like youthful wanderers for the first time free—
Hear you the lovely and funereal voice
That sings: 'O come all ye whose wandering joys

'Are set upon the scented Lotus flower,
For here we sell the fruit's miraculous boon;
Come ye and drink the sweet and sleepy power
Of the enchanted, endless afternoon.'*

*See *Notes* on no. CLI, page 201.

VIII

O Death, old Captain, it is time, put forth!
We have grown weary of the gloomy north;
Though sea and sky are black as ink, lift sail!
Our hearts are full of light and will not fail.

O pour thy sleepy poison in the cup!
The fire within the heart so burns us up
That we would wander Hell and Heaven through,
Deep in the Unknown seeking something *new!*

[JAMES HUNEKER]

Condemned Poems

CLII

The Jewels

Naked the loved one lay, and as she knows
My heart, she kept her tinkling jewels on,
Whose richness lent the conquering mien of those
Proud captives of the Moors in days long gone.

When jingling sharply, mockingly it moves—
This world of metal and of shining stone—
My heart's ecstatic, for it madly loves
Mingled degrees of light and music's tone.

She let me love her, languid as she lay,
And from the high divan smiled down at me;
And my love mounted to her, as the spray
Climbs up the cliff's face from the unfathomed sea.

Like a tamed beast, she gazed at me and dreamed,
Trying new attitudes, now these, now those,
And Innocence, wed to Love's Learning, seemed
To give new charm to every change of pose.

Her arms, her oil-smooth limbs, her hips, her thighs,
Moved like a swan their undulating line,
Before my pensive and clairvoyant eyes;
Her breasts, her belly, ripe fruits of Love's vine,

Offered themselves, like angels out of Hell,
To trouble my tranquillity of mind,
And tempt it from its crystal citadel,
Where solitude and peace it hoped to find.

In one new shape, my curious eyes observe
Antiope's proud hips, most strangely blent
With a boy's breast—so sharp the body's curve.
On that dark skin rouge was magnificent!

And as the lamp resigned itself to die,
And only firelight lit the scene of sin,
Each time it flamed into a final sigh
It flushed with blood the amber-coloured skin.

[JAMES LAVER]

CLIII

Lethe

Come to my heart, cold, cruel concubine,
Beloved tiger, hydra indolent;
Long will I drag my hands incontinent
And quivering, through that heavy mane of thine;

Long will I hide my aching brows and head
Amid thy skirts so redolent of thee,
And breathe, a withered flower of memory,
The fading perfume of my passion dead.

For I shall sleep!—forget life's clarions
In slumber soft as Death's ambiguous shore,
I'll sleep, and sow my drowsy kisses o'er
Thy beauteous body polished bright as bronze.

To drown my sobbing soul in silence,—Oh!
Thy bed alone, vile paramour, avails;
Poppied oblivion from thy mouth exhales,
And through thy kisses floods of Lethe flow.

So to my doom or rather my desire,
I shall submit as one predestinate;
And like a martyr, calm, immaculate,
Whose fervour stirs the flames as they expire,

I'll drain, to drown my rancour and my smart,
Death's bitter hemlock and Nepenthe blest,
That sleep within the rose-buds of thy breast,
Thy lovely breast that ne'er contained a heart.

[LEWIS PIAGET SHANKS]

CLIV

A Girl Too Gay

Oh, you are lovely! Every heart
Surrenders to your sorceries;
And laughter, like a playful breeze,
Is always blowing your lips apart.

Your health is radiant, infinite,
Superb: When you go down the street
Each mournful passer-by you meet
Is dazzled by the blaze of it!

Your startling dresses, overwrought
With rainbow hues and sequined showers,
Bring to a poet's mind the thought
Of a ballet of drunken flowers.

They are the very symbol of
Your gay and crudely coloured soul,
As stripèd as a barber's pole,
Exuberant thing I hate and love!

Sometimes when wandering, full of gloom,
In a bright garden, I have felt
Horror for all I touched and smelt:
The world outrageously in bloom,

The blinding yellow sun, the spring's
Raw verdure so rebuked my woes
That I have punished upon a rose
The insolence of flowering things.

Likewise, some evening, I would creep,
When midnight sounds, and everywhere
The sighing of lovers fills the air,
To the hushed alcove where you sleep,

And waken you by violent storm,
And beat you coldly till you swooned,
And carve upon your perfect form,
With care, a deep seductive wound—

And (joy delirious and complete!)
Through those bright novel lips, through this
Gaudy and virgin orifice,
Infuse you with my venom, sweet.

[GEORGE DILLON]

CLV

Lesbos

Mother of Latin revelry and of Greek delight,
Lesbos, whereof the kisses, disconsolate or gay,
Hot as the sun, or cool as melons plucked by night,
Beguile the unshadowed and the shadowed hours away;
Mother of Latin revelry and of Greek delight,

Lesbos, whereof the kisses are whirlpools and cascades
Journeying carelessly into a dark abyss:
So wild the sobbing and laughter among thy colonnades,
So secret, so profound, so stormy, every kiss!
Lesbos, whereof the kisses are whirlpools and cascades!

Lesbos, where the sweet slaves one to another yearn,
Where there is never a glance without an echoing sign;
Even as upon Cyprus the stars upon thee burn
With praise, and Cyprus' queen is envious of thine,
Lesbos, where the sweet slaves one to another yearn—

Lesbos, of sultry twilights and pure, infertile joy,
Where deep-eyed maidens, thoughtlessly disrobing, see
Their beauty, and are entranced before their mirrors,
    and toy
Fondly with the soft fruits of their nubility;
Lesbos, of sultry twilights and pure, infertile joy!

Let frown the old lined forehead of Plato as it will:
Thy pardon is assured—even by the strange excess,
Luxurious isle, of thy long sterile rapture, still
Contriving some new freak or form of tenderness;
Let frown the old lined forehead of Plato as it will.

Thy pardon has been bought with our eternal pain,
The lonely martyrdom endured in every age
By those who sigh for pleasures outlandish and insane
To ease the unearthly longing no pleasure can assuage.
Thy pardon has been bought with our eternal pain.

Who, Lesbos, of the gods would dare pronounce thy fate
And brand thy passionate white brow with infamy—
Or hope by any art or science to estimate
The tears, the tears thy streams have poured into the sea?
Who, Lesbos, of the gods would dare pronounce thy fate?

What are men's laws to us, injurious or benign?
Proud virgins, glory of the Ægean! We know well
Love, be it most foredoomed, most desperate, is divine,
And love will always laugh at heaven and at hell!
What are men's laws to us, injurious or benign?

Lo! I was named by Lesbos of all the lists of earth
To celebrate her sad-eyed girls and their sweet lore:
And I have known from childhood the noise of loud,
    crazed mirth
Confused mysteriously with terrible weeping—for
Lo! I was named by Lesbos of all the lists of earth.

And I have watched thenceforward from the
    Leucadian cliff,
Like an unwearying old sentry, who can descry
Far out on the horizon a sailboat or a skiff
Invisible to others, with his sharp, practised eye;
And I have watched thenceforward from the
    Leucadian cliff

To find if the cold wave were pitiful and good—
And someday I shall see come wandering home, I know,
To all-forgiving Lesbos upon the twilight flood
The sacred ruins of Sappho, who set forth long ago
To find if the cold wave were pitiful and good;

Of Sappho, poet and lover—the virile, calm, and brave,
More beautiful than Venus, by force of earthly grief—
More beautiful than blue-eyed Venus, with her grave
And dusky glance disclosing the sorrows past belief
Of Sappho, poet and lover—the virile, calm, and brave:

More beautiful than Venus arising to the world
And scattering all round her the iridescent fire
Of her blond loveliness with rainbow hues impearled
Upon the old green ocean, her bedazzled sire;
More beautiful than Venus arising to the world!

—Of Sappho, who died proudly the day of her soul's
    crime
When, faithless to her teaching and to her serious pledge,
She flung the occult dark roses of her love sublime
To a vain churl. Alas! How deep the sacrilege
Of Sappho, who died proudly the day of her soul's crime!

And from that day to this the isle of Lesbos mourns—
And heedful of the world's late homage in no wise,
Gives answer but with the hollow moaning of her
    wild bourns:
The sea's long obloquy to the unlistening skies!
And from that day to this the isle of Lesbos mourns.

[GEORGE DILLON]

CLVI

Damned Women

The lamps had languisht and their light was pale;
On cushions deep Hippolyta reclined.
Those potent kisses that had torn the veil
From her young candour filled her dreaming mind.

With tempest-troubled eyes she sought the blue
Heaven of her innocence, how far away!
Like some sad traveller, who turns to view
The dim horizons passed at dawn of day.

Tears and the muffled light of weary eyes,
The stupor and the dull voluptuous trance,
Limp arms, like weapons dropped by one who flies—
All served her fragile beauty to enhance.

Calm at her feet and joyful, Delphine lay
And gazed at her with ardent eyes and bright,
Like some strong beast that, having mauled its prey,
Draws back to mark the imprint of its bite.

Strong and yet bowed, superbly on her knees,
She snuffed her triumph, on that frailer grace
Poring voluptuously, as though to seize
The signs of thanks upon the other's face.

Gazing, she sought in her pale victim's eye
The speechless canticle that pleasure sings,
The infinite gratitude that, like a sigh,
Mounts slowly from the spirit's deepest springs.

'Now, now you understand (for love like ours
Is proof enough) that 'twere a sin to throw
The sacred holocaust of your first flowers
To those whose breath might parch them as they blow.

'Light falls my kiss, as the ephemeral wing
That scarcely stirs the shining of a lake.
What ruinous pain your lover's kiss would bring!
A plough that leaves a furrow in its wake.

'Over you, like a herd of ponderous kine,
Man's love will pass and his caresses fall
Like trampling hooves. Then turn your face to mine;
Turn, oh my heart, my half of me, my all!

'Turn, turn, that I may see their starry lights,
Your eyes of azure; turn. For one dear glance
I will reveal love's most obscure delights,
And you shall drowse in pleasure's endless trance.'

'Not thankless, nor repentant in the least
Is your Hippolyta.' She raised her head.
'But one who from some grim nocturnal feast
Returns at dawn feels less disquieted.

'I bear a weight of terrors, and dark hosts
Of phantoms haunt my steps and seem to lead.
I walk, compelled, behind these beckoning ghosts
Down sliding roads and under skies that bleed.

'Is ours so strange an act, so full of shame?
Explain the terrors that disturb my bliss.
When you say, Love, I tremble at the name;
And yet my mouth is thirsty for your kiss.

'Ah, look not so, dear sister, look not so!
You whom I love, even though that love should be
A snare for my undoing, even though
Loving I am lost for all eternity.'

Delphine looked up, and fate was in her eye.
From the god's tripod and beneath his spell,
Shaking her tragic locks, she made reply:
'Who in love's presence dares to speak of hell?

'Thinker of useless thoughts, let him be cursed,
Who in his folly, venturing to vex
A question answerless and barren, first
With wrong and right involved the things of sex!

'He who in mystical accord conjoins
Shadow with heat, dusk with the noon's high fire,
Shall never warm the palsy of his loins
At that red sun which mortals call desire.

'Go, seek some lubber groom's deflowering lust;
Take him your heart and leave me here despised!
Go—and bring back, all horror and disgust,
The livid breasts man's love has stigmatized.

'One may not serve two masters here below.'
But the child answered: 'I am torn apart,
I feel my inmost being rent, as though
A gulf had yawned—the gulf that is my heart.

'Naught may this monster's desperate thirst assuage,—
As fire 'tis hot, as space itself profound—
Naught stay the Fury from her quenchless rage,
Who with her torch explores its bleeding wound.

'Curtain the world away and let us try
If lassitude will bring the boon of rest.
In your deep bosom I would sink and die,
Would find the grave's fresh coolness on your breast.'

Hence, lamentable victims, get you hence!
Hell yawns beneath, your road is straight and steep.
Where all the crimes receive their recompense
Wind-whipped and seething in the lowest deep

With a huge roaring as of storms and fires,
Go down, mad phantoms, doomed to seek in vain
The ne'er-won goal of unassuaged desires,
And in your pleasures find eternal pain!

Sunless your caverns are; the fever damps
That filter in through every crannied vent
Break out with marsh-fire into sudden lamps
And steep your bodies with their frightful scent.

The barrenness of pleasures harsh and stale
Makes mad your thirst and parches up your skin;
And like an old flag volleying in the gale,
Your whole flesh shudders in the blasts of sin.

Far from your kind, outlawed and reprobate,
Go, prowl like wolves through desert worlds apart!
Disordered souls, fashion your own dark fate,
And flee the god you carry in your heart.

[ALDOUS HUXLEY]

CLVII

Metamorphoses of the Vampire

Meanwhile from her red mouth the woman, in
     husky tones,
Twisting her body like a serpent upon hot stones
And straining her white breasts from their imprisonment,
Let fall these words, as potent as a heavy scent:
'My lips are moist and yielding, and I know the way
To keep the antique demon of remorse at bay.
All sorrows die upon my bosom. I can make
Old men laugh happily as children for my sake.
For him who sees me naked in my tresses, I
Replace the sun, the moon, and all the stars of the sky!
Believe me, learnèd sir, I am so deeply skilled
That when I wind a lover in my soft arms, and yield
My breasts like two ripe fruits for his devouring—both
Shy and voluptuous, insatiable and loath—
Upon this bed that groans and sighs luxuriously
Even the impotent angels would be damned for me!'

When she had drained me of my very marrow, and cold
And weak, I turned to give her one more kiss—behold,
There at my side was nothing but a hideous
Putrescent thing, all faceless and exuding pus.
I closed my eyes and mercifully swooned till day:
And when I looked at morning for that beast of prey
Who seemed to have replenished her arteries from
    my own,
The wan, disjointed fragments of a skeleton
Wagged up and down in a lewd posture where she
    had lain,
Rattling with each convulsion like a weathervane
Or an old sign that creaks upon its bracket, right
Mournfully in the wind upon a winter's night.

[GEORGE DILLON]

Loin des peuples vivants,
A travers les déserts
Cour...
Faites votre destin...
Et fuyez l'infini...
qu...

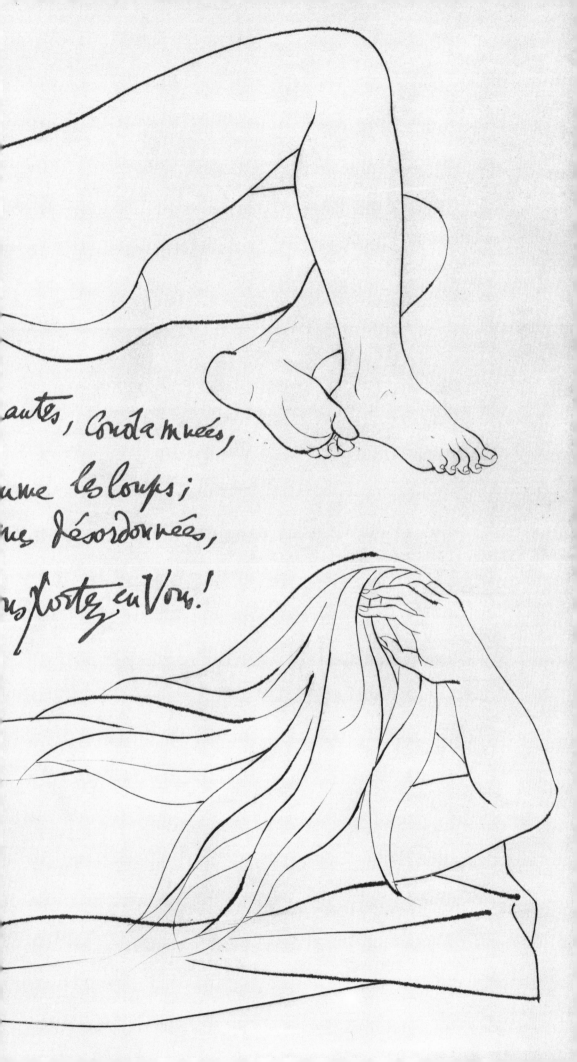

autes, Condamnées,

me les loups;

us désordonnées,

us portez en Vous!

Additional Poems

CLVIII

What a Pair of Eyes Can Promise

I love, pale one, your lifted eyebrows bridging
    Twin darknesses of flowing depth.
But however deep they are, they carry me
    Another way than that of death.

Your eyes, doubly echoing your hair's darkness
    —That leaping, running mane—
Your eyes, though languidly, instruct me: 'Poet
    And connoisseur of love made plain,

'If you desire fulfilment of the promise,
    The ecstasy that is your trade,
You can confirm the truth, from thigh to navel,
    Of all that we have said.

'You will find my white breasts heavy
    With the weight of their rough, bronze coins,
And, under a soft as velvet, rounded belly,
    Poised between ambered loins,

'A fleece, not golden, but for richness sister
    To that hair with darkness bright,
Supple and springing—and as boundless
    As a deep, starless night!'

[DAVID PAUL]

CLIX

The Paranymph

I

No, my dear, you're certainly not
What some might call a dainty dish.
You simmer like an ancient pot
With leavings of lust, and worldly relish.
Fresh and sweet you're certainly not,

My raddled old infanta! Yet
The cavortings of your crazy career
Have given you the greasy sweat
Of things worn out with common wear,
Which hold their tattered value yet.

The green sap of your forty years
Has a tang to wake the jaded palate.
The ripe old fruit that autumn bears
Makes all spring's virgin bloom look pallid!
—There's plenty of sap in your forty years!

Your carcase has its peculiar charms,
Little graces all its own.
Your pepper-pots give me the qualms
—But the flesh is sweetest near the bone!
Yes, your carcase has its charms!

Cock a snook at the connoisseurs
Of the pumpkin and the watermelon!
I'd rather those collarbones of yours
Than all the Songs of Solomon,
—And I'm sorry for those connoisseurs!

You wear your hair like a blue helmet,
Hanging over your blushless brow,
Swathing your empty head with its pelmet

—And then at the back it lifts its prow
Like the plumes of a blue helmet!

Your eyes are black as a street puddle
Catching the glitter of a lamp.
Against the rouge on your cheekbone's middle
They shine with the threat of Hell's fire-damp,
And yet they're black as a street puddle.

The curl of your lip lures and shocks
With its lech, and its look of 'You keep out!'
Like the Tree of Knowledge it provokes
The longing to know what we'd better not!
Yes, the lust in you both lures and shocks.

Your legs are sinewy enough
To scale the heights of a volcano,
And, rain or snow, in cold or cough,
To dance a can-can as only they know
Whose legs are hard and dry enough.

Your skin is hot, and quite as sweet
As that of a seasoned brigadier,
And it's as innocent of sweat
As your eyes are of a tear
—And yet, and yet I've found it sweet!

II

Deviless, you're heading for the devil!
I'd gladly keep you company,
If only the pace at which you travel
Didn't leave me somewhat dizzy.
So get on, alone, with you to the Devil!

My sciatica, asthma, rheumatism
Won't let me render as I ought
His Lordship's homage, without a spasm.
'Now isn't that a shame!' cry out
My asthma and my rheumatism.

Oh you can't guess how much I suffer
To miss your sabbatical conference.
To watch you, when he lets go his sulphur
Kissing his royal circumstance!
Yes, truly and indeed I suffer!

It's damnably sad to bid farewell
To you, my dear, at such a juncture.
No more, my old flambeau of Hell,
To be your holder! Judge what torture
It is, my dear, to say farewell,

For you've been my passion many a year,
A passion sufficiently logical!
I wanted to skim the cream, my dear,
Of all that could be perfectly evil.
—My monster, I've loved you many a year.

[DAVID PAUL]

CLX

Amina Boschetti

Amina bounds . . . is startled . . . whirls and smiles.
The Belgian says, 'That's fraud, a pure deceit.
As for your woodland nymphs, I know the wiles
Only of those on Brussels' Market Street.'

From shapely foot and lively, laughing eye
Amina spills light elegance and wit.
The Belgian says, 'Be gone, ye joys that fly!
My wife's attractions have more solid merit.'

Oh, you forget, nymph of the winsome stance,
That though you'd teach an elephant to dance,
Teach owls new melodies, make dull birds shine,

All glimmering grace brings but a Belgian sneer:
Bacchus himself could pour bright southern wine,
This Boor would say, 'Give me thick Brussels beer.'

[KENNETH O. HANSON]

CLXI

About a Bore Who Claimed His Acquaintance

TO M. EUGÈNE FROMENTIN

He told me just how rich he was,
But nervous of the cholera;
—That he took good care where the money goes,
But he liked a seat at the Opera.

—That he was simply wild about nature,
Monsieur Corot being quite an old chum;
—That a carriage was still a missing feature
Among his goods—but it would come;

—That marble and brick divided his fancy,
Along with ebony and gilded wood;
—That there were in his factory
Three foremen who had been decorated;

—That, not to mention all the rest,
He had twenty thousand shares in the *Nord;*
—That he'd found some picture-frames for next
To nothing, and all by Oppenord;

—That he'd go as far even as Luzarches
To steep himself in bric-à-brac;
—That the Marché des Patriarches
Had more than once proved his collector's knack;

—That he didn't care much for his wife
Nor for his mother, but—theirs apart—
He believed in the soul's immortal life.
Niboyet's works he *had* by heart!

—That he quite approved of physical passion,
And once, on a tedious stay in Rome,
A consumptive lady, much in fashion,
Had died away for love of him.

—For three solid hours and a half,
This chatterer, born in Tournai,
Dished up to me the whole of his life,
Until my brain almost fainted away.

If I had to tell you all I suffered
I would never be able to give up.
I sat in helpless hate, and muttered
'If only I could lie down and sleep!'

Like someone whose seat can give no rest
But who cannot get up and make his escape,
I squirmed and brooded on all the best
Methods of torturing the ape.

Bastogne this monstrosity's called;
He was running away from the infection.
I would drown myself, or take the road
To Gascony, or in any direction

If, when everybody gets back
To the Paris he's so much afraid of,
I should happen to cross the track
Of this pest that Tournai bore—and got rid of!
                              Brussels, 1865

[DAVID PAUL]

CLXII

A Gay Chophouse

(ON THE ROAD FROM BRUSSELS TO UCCLE)

You who adore the skeleton
And all such horrible devices
As so many relishes and spices
To tickle the delicate palate on,

You old Pharaoh, Monselet,
Here's a sign I saw that will surely whet
Your appetite for an omelette;
It read: *Cemetery View. Estaminet.*

[DAVID PAUL]

Notes

NOTES TO THE POEMS

TO THE READER. First appeared under this title as the first of seventeen poems in *La Revue des Deux-Mondes*, June 1st, 1855. The title was changed to *Préface* in the later editions of the collected poems.

I. The poem expresses Baudelaire's horror at his mother's remarriage.

II. A recollection of an incident during Baudelaire's voyage to Mauritius (1841). The poem originally consisted of three stanzas only, the two first and the last. The other was added on the advice of Asselineau. Baudelaire is said to have recited the poem to friends soon after his return to Paris. The poem first appeared in *La Revue Française*, April 10th, 1859, and was reproduced in *Les Poètes Français*, published by E. Crépet, 1862. The other poems, inspired by Baudelaire's stay in Mauritius, were *A une dame créole*, *A une Malabaraise*, and *Bien loin d'ici*.

IV. Some critics have detected in the first stanza an echo of two lines in Poe's *Al Aaraaf*:

> *All Nature speaks, and e'en ideal things*
> *Flap shadowy sounds from visionary wings.*

IX. One of the earliest of the poems. Baudelaire gave a copy to his friend Auguste Dozon in 1842 or 1843. First published in *Le Messager de l'Assemblée*, April 9th, 1851, with ten other poems under the title *Les Limbes*.

X. First published in *La Revue des Deux-Mondes*, June 1st, 1855.

XI. Baudelaire originally thought of calling this poem *L'artiste inconnu*. It was inspired partly by Longfellow's *A Psalm of Life*:

> *Art is long, and Time is fleeting,*
> *And our hearts, though stout and brave,*
> *Still, like muffled drums, are beating*
> *Funeral marches to the grave.*

And partly by Gray's *Elegy Written in a Country Churchyard*:

> *Full many a gem of purest ray serene*
> *The dark, unfathomed caves of ocean bear;*

Full many a flower is born to blush unseen,
And waste its sweetness on the desert air.

It was sent to Gautier in 1852, and was first published in *La Revue des Deux-Mondes*, June 1st, 1855.

XII. First published in *La Revue des Deux-Mondes*, June 1st, 1855.

XIII. Known to have been written in or before 1852.

XIV. First published in *La Revue de Paris*, October, 1852.

XV. According to Prarond, the poem existed before 1843. It was probably inspired by the painting *La Barque de Don Juan* of Delacroix (1841). First published under the title *L'Impénitent* in *L'Artiste*, December 6th, 1846.

XVI. This poem does not appear in the first or second editions of *Les Fleurs du Mal*. Banville's *Les Cariatides* had been published in 1842 and was much admired by Baudelaire.

XVII. First published in *Le Musée des Familles*, No. 10, 1850.

XVIII. First published in *La Revue Française*, April 20th, 1857.

XIX. First published in *Le Messager de l'Assemblée*, April 9th, 1851.

XX. Baudelaire's passion for the extraordinary led him to envisage with pleasure sexual intercourse with dwarfs and giantesses. He regretted that these creatures should so often be delicate in health and professed to have "lost" several giantesses through tuberculosis and two dwarfs through gastritis. There was no doubt an element of mystification in all this, and his relations with very big or very small women may be assumed to have been largely imaginary. According to Prarond, Baudelaire's youthful friend at the Pension Bailly, this poem was written before 1843. It was first published in *La Revue Française*, April 20th, 1857.

XXI. Inspired by a statue by Ernest Christophe entitled first *La Douleur* and later *La Comédie Humaine*, exhibited in the Salon of 1856 and now in the Garden of the Tuileries. First published in *La Revue Contemporaine*, November 30th, 1859.

XXII. First published in *L'Artiste*, October 15th, 1860.

XXIII. Inspired by Jeanne Duval, the poet's coloured mistress, but with memories also of his voyage to Mauritius, and of Dorothée. (See note on XCII.)

XXIV. Inspired by Jeanne Duval. First published in *La Revue Française*, May 20th, 1859.

XXV. Inspired by Jeanne Duval (and her known infidelities to the poet). According to Prarond, composed about 1843.

XXVI. Inspired by Jeanne Duval.

XXVII. Inspired by Jeanne Duval. Probably composed in 1843 or 1844. The title means "But unsatiated"; cf. Juvenal, *Satire* VI: *lassata nondum satiata recessit* ('wearied, yet not sated, she withdrew'), describing Messalina leaving the brothel.

XXVIII. Inspired by Jeanne Duval. First published in *La Revue Française,* April 20th, 1857.

XXIX. Inspired by Jeanne Duval.

XXX. According to Prarond, the poem was composed before 1844.

XXXI. Published under the title *La Béatrix* in *Le Messager de l'Assemblée*, April 9th, 1851, and as *Spleen* in *La Revue des Deux-Mondes,* June 1st, 1855. The final version of the title means "I called out from the depths."

XXXII. Inspired by Jeanne Duval.

XXXIII. One of the earliest poems, according to Prarond, who identifies the "juive" as one Sarah, called "Louchette," who was Baudelaire's mistress before Jeanne Duval.

XXXIV. Probably inspired by Jeanne Duval. First published in *La Revue des Deux-Mondes,* June 1st, 1855.

XXXV. Perhaps inspired by Jeanne Duval.

XXXVI. Probably inspired by Jeanne Duval. First published in *L'Artiste,* September 19th, 1858.

XXXVII. Probably inspired by Jeanne Duval.

XXXVIII. Apparently inspired by Jeanne Duval, and seemingly written in 1858. First published in *La Revue Française*, January 20th, 1859.

XXXIX. Composed in 1860. The *fantôme* is probably Jeanne Duval, who at that date was half-paralysed, having undermined her health by alcohol. The four sonnets were first published in *L'Artiste*, October 15th, 1860.

XL. Inspired by Jeanne Duval. First published in *La Revue Française*, April 20th, 1857.

XLI. Probably inspired by Madame Sabatier. Jacques Crépet (*Œuvres Complètes de Charles Baudelaire,* 1922) believes that this poem should be added to "Le Cycle de Mme. Sabatier" which consisted, according to Baudelaire himself, of *Tout entière, Que diras-tu ce soir, Le Flambeau vivant, A celle qui est trop gaie, Réversibilité, Confession, L'Aube spirituelle, Harmonie du Soir* and *Le Flacon,* to which is usually added *Hymne.* First published in *La Revue Contemporaine,* May 15th, 1860.

XLII. Inspired by Madame Sabatier. First published in *La Revue Française,* April 20th, 1857.

XLIII. Inspired by Madame Sabatier and sent to her February 16th, 1854.

XLIV. Inspired by Madame Sabatier and sent to her February 7th, 1854. First published in *La Revue Française,* April 20th, 1857.

XLV. Inspired by Madame Sabatier and sent to her anonymously May 3rd, 1853. First published in *La Revue des Deux-Mondes,* June 1st, 1855.

XLVI. Inspired by Madame Sabatier and sent to her May 9th, 1853. First published in *La Revue des Deux-Mondes,* June 1st, 1859.

XLVII. Inspired by Madame Sabatier and sent to her in February, 1854. First published in *La Revue des Deux-Mondes,* June 1st, 1855.

XLVIII. Inspired by Madame Sabatier. First published in *La Revue Française,* April 20th, 1857.

XLIX. Inspired by Madame Sabatier. First published in *La Revue Française,* April 20th, 1857.

L. First published in *La Revue Française,* April 20th, 1857.

LIII. Inspired by Jeanne Duval.

LIV. First published in *La Revue des Deux-Mondes,* June 1st, 1855.

LV. Inspired by Madame Marie Brunaud, called Daubrun, who played the part of *La Belle aux cheveux d'or* at the Théâtre de la Porte-Saint-Martin in 1853. First published under the title *A la Belle aux cheveux d'or* in *La Revue des Deux-Mondes,* June 1st, 1855.

LVI. Apparently inspired by Marie Daubrun.

LVII. Apparently inspired by Marie Daubrun, and dedicated to her, under the initials "M.D." in 1859. First published in *La Revue Contemporaine,* November 30th, 1859.

LVIII. Probably written for Marie Daubrun, who was blonde and had a

Madonna-like face, and possibly inspired by a passage in *The Monk*, by Matthew Gregory Lewis. The monk, Ambrosio, has in his cell an image of the Madonna and has never seen any other woman. The devil, to tempt him, sends to his cell a woman exactly similar to the image. Ambrosio falls, and in fury breaks the image. First published in *La Causerie*, January 22nd, 1860.

LIX. Apparently inspired by Jeanne Duval. First published in *L'Artiste*, October 15th, 1860.

LX. Inspired by Sisina Nieri, friend of Madame Sabatier and a well-known beauty of the Second Empire. She professed herself a Republican and an admirer of Orsini, who attempted to assassinate Napoleon III. Anne Josephe Théroigne de Méricourt (1762-1817), to whom Sisina is compared, was a female orator and leader of the mob during the French Revolution. She was known as the "Fury of the Gironde." First published in *La Revue Française*, April 10th, 1859.

LXI. Champfleury, being about to publish his *Histoire de la Caricature moderne*, wrote to Baudelaire in May, 1865, and asked him for some verses to be placed under the engraved portrait of Daumier by Pascal. Baudelaire, who was, as Champfleury remarked, *"plein de Daumier,"* sent the verses by return of post.

LXII. To this poem, dedicated to *"une modiste érudite et dévote,"* Baudelaire added the following curious note: "Does it not seem to the reader, as to me, that the language of the late Latin Decadence — the final sigh of a robust creature already transformed and ready for the spiritual life — is singularly apt to express passion as it is understood and felt in modern poetry? Mysticism is the other pole of that love of which Catullus and his band, brutal and purely epidermic poets, knew only the pole of sensuality. In this wonderful language, the solecism and the barbarism seem to me to render admirably the inevitable negligences of a passion which forgets itself and mocks at rules. The words, taken in a new sense, reveal the charming awkwardness of the northern barbarian on his knees before the beauty of Rome. Even the pun, when it slips into these pedantic stammerings, has something of the rude, baroque grace of childhood." The title means "In praise of my Françoise."

LXIII. Written by Baudelaire in his twenty-first year (1841) and inspired by Madame Autard de Bragard, mother of the Countess Ferdinand de Lesseps, during his enforced stay in Mauritius. It was his first printed poem, and was published under the title *A une Créole* in *L'Artiste*, May 24th, 1845.

LXIV. Agathe is unidentified. First published in *La Revue des Deux-Mondes*, June 1st, 1855. The title means "Sad, wandering one."

LXV. Possibly inspired by Jeanne Duval.

LXVI. Believed by Jacques Crépet (*op. cit.*) to refer, under the name of Marguerite, to Marie Daubrun, who played Margue in *Le Sanglier des Ardennes* at the Théâtre de la Gaieté, in 1854, by which time she may, in Baudelaire's eyes, have lost her youth and have been no longer *La Belle aux cheveux d'or*. (See note on LV.) It was first published in *La Revue Contemporaine*, November 30th, 1859.

LXVII. Written before 1850.

LXVIII. First published without the name of the author by Champfleury in his *feuilleton Le Corsaire*, November 14th, 1847. Published under Baudelaire's name in *Le Messager de l'Assemblée*, April 9th, 1851.

LXIX. First published in *Le Messager de l'Assemblée*, April 9th, 1851, and in *Les Poètes Français*, 1862.

LXXII. Called in the posthumous edition *The Burial of an Accursed Poet*. This is probably an error as the phrase *"votre corps vanté"* seems to imply that the body was that of a woman.

LXXIII. First published under the title *Une gravure de Mortimer* in *Le Présent*, November 15th, 1857. John Hamilton Mortimer (1741-1779) was an English painter and engraver of historical and legendary subjects, with a marked taste for the horrific.

LXXIV. First published in *Le Messager de l'Assemblée*, April 9th, 1851.

LXXV. Written before 1850. Published in *Le Messager de l'Assemblée*, April 9th, 1851, and in *La Revue des Deux-Mondes*, June 1st, 1855.

LXXVI. First published under the title *Spleen* in *Le Messager de l'Assemblée*, April 9th, 1851, and as *La Cloche* in *La Revue des Deux-Mondes*, June 1st, 1855.

LXXVII–LXXX. First published in *Le Messager de l'Assemblée*, April 9th, 1851.

LXXXI. First published in *La Revue Contemporaine*, May 15th, 1860.

LXXXII. Baudelaire was now beginning to be conscious of the first signs of approaching imbecility. First published in *La Revue Française*, January 20th, 1859.

LXXXIII–LXXXIV. First published in *L'Artiste*, October 15th, 1860.

LXXXV. These verses were translated from Longfellow's *Hiawatha* at the end of 1860 and were intended to be recited during the intervals of the performance of a symphony by Robert Stoepel. This project was never realised. The verses were first published in *La Revue Contemporaine*, February 28th, 1861, and included in the "definitive" edition of *Les Fleurs du Mal*, 1868.

LXXXVI. Published in *La Revue européenne*, September 15th, 1861, and in *Le Boulevard*, January 12th, 1862.

LXXXVII. Published in *Le Boulevard*, January 12th, 1862, and in *Le Parnasse contemporain*, 1866.

LXXXVIII. First published in *Le Boulevard*, February 25th, 1863, where the poem is dedicated to Barbey d'Aurevilly.

LXXXIX. Published in *Le Boulevard*, February 1st, 1863, and in *Le Parnasse contemporain*, 1866.

XC. Possibly inspired by Jeanne Duval. Published in *La Revue fantaisiste*, May 15th, 1861, and in *Le Parnasse contemporain*, 1866.

XCI. Published in *La Revue européenne*, September 15th, 1861, in *Le Boulevard*, January 12th, 1862, and in *Le Parnasse contemporain*, 1866.

XCII. Presumably inspired by a coloured prostitute in Paris, but so full of memories of "*La Belle Dorothée*" that it may be considered to belong to her "cycle." Dorothée, a pretty *malabaraise*, the daughter of an Indian woman from Benares, was the foster-sister of Madame Autard de Bragard and as a servant in her house in Mauritius served Baudelaire and is thought by some to have been his mistress. (See also XCIX; XXIII, although inspired by Jeanne Duval, is also full of memories of Dorothée.) Published in *L'Artiste*, December 13th, 1846, in *Le Présent*, November 15th, 1857, in *La Petite Revue*, October 14th, 1855, and in *Le Parnasse contemporain*, 1866.

XCIII. Published in *La Revue contemporaine*, February 28th, 1861, in *L'Artiste*, March 1st, 1862, and in *Le Parnasse contemporain*, 1866.

XCIV. Inspired by Madame Sabatier and sent to her with an anonymous letter, May 8th, 1854. Published in *Le Présent*, November 15th, 1857, in *La Petite Revue*, December 16th, 1865, and in *Le Parnasse contemporain*, 1866. The title means "The unknown god."

XCV. According to Prarond, written before 1843. Published in *La Revue européenne*, September 15th, 1861, in *Le Boulevard*, January 12th, 1862, and in *Le Parnasse contemporain*, 1866.

XCVI. Prarond declares the poem to have been written before the end of 1843, but it is now generally believed to date from 1864 when the poet, in Brussels, tried to adopt a girl called Berthe without knowing anything either of the law of adoption or of the character of his protégée. Baudelaire would seem to have been a most unsuitable person to adopt anybody, and that the experiment was not a success may be judged from his own description of the girl as "*une horrible petite folle.*" Published in *La Revue nouvelle*, March 1st, 1864, and in *Le Parnasse contemporain*, 1866.

XCVII. The poem was written before 1853. It was set to music by Rollinat. Published in *La Petite Revue*, July 8th, 1865, and in *Le Parnasse contemporain*, 1866.

XCVIII. Published in *Le Présent*, November 15th, 1857, in *La Petite Revue*, December 16th, 1865, and in *Le Parnasse contemporain*, 1866.

XCIX. The poem seems to have been composed in 1859 and was perhaps first called *Dorothée*. (See note on XCII.) Published in *La Revue nouvelle*, March 1st, 1864, and in *Le Parnasse contemporain*, 1866.

C. Published in *Le Boulevard*, January 12th, 1862, in *L'Almanach parisien*, 1863, and in Fernand Desnoyer's *Mélanges tirés d'une petite bibliothèque romantique*, 1867. It formed the first poem of *Les Epaves*.

CI. The poem is thought to have been written in 1844 and to have been inspired by Delacroix's painting exhibited in the Galeries des Beaux Arts of the Bazar Bonne-Nouvelle. It was sent to the editor of the *Bulletin de l'Ami des Arts*, which, however, ceased publication before the poem was inserted. Published in *La Revue nouvelle*, March 1st, 1864.

CII. Published in *L'Artiste*, March 1st, 1862, in *La Revue nouvelle*, March 1st, 1864, and in *Le Parnasse contemporain*, 1866.

CIII. Published in *Le Boulevard*, December 28th, 1862, and in *Le Parnasse contemporain*, 1866.

CIV. The poem was put to music by Villiers de l'Isle-Adam. Published in *La Revue européenne*, November 1st, 1861, in *Le Boulevard*, January 12th, 1862, and in *Le Parnasse contemporain*, 1866.

CV. The title of "Self-Executioner" is that of a play by Terence, but Jacques Crépet (*op. cit.*) thinks that it is borrowed here from a phrase in Joseph de Maistre's *Soirées de Saint-Petersbourg: "en vertu de lois seules que Dieu a portées avec tant de sagesse, tout méchant est un héautontimorouménos."* The dedication to J. G. F. was added in the second edition, and the same dedication appears at the beginning of *Les Paradis Artificiels*. It is not known what the initials signify.

CVI. Certain images in the poem are thought to have been suggested by Poe's *Manuscript Found in a Bottle* and *Descent into the Maelstrom*. First published in *L'Artiste*, May 10th, 1857. In the second edition the poem was divided into two parts, the second part being formed by the last two stanzas.

CVII. First published in *L'Artiste*, October 15th, 1860.

CVIII. Thought to have been written after 1852 when Baudelaire lost interest in the democratic movement. First published under the title *Paysage parisien* in *Le Présent*, November 15th, 1857.

CX. Lola de Valence was a dancer belonging to a troupe of Spanish singers and dancers visiting Paris. Manet painted his famous portrait of her in 1862 and Baudelaire, who had constituted himself the painter's champion, composed the poem in its honour.

CXI. Published in *L'Artiste*, March 1st, 1862.

CXII. This poem, which was already in existence, according to Cousin, in 1842, was composed in honour of a young girl who sang and played the guitar in the Paris cafés. Théodore de Banville wrote verses to her and described her appearance in his *Souvenirs*. Her portrait was painted by Emile Deroy, an artist of brilliant promise who died in 1848, aged 23. He also painted, at the age of nineteen, a portrait of Baudelaire, aged 20, which is now in the Versailles Museum.

CXIII. Published in *La Revue Contemporaine* in 1859 and in *La Causerie*, January 22nd, 1860.

CXIV. Published in *La Revue Contemporaine*, September 15th, 1859, and in *L'Artiste*, January 15th, 1861.

CXV. Published in *La Revue Contemporaine*, September 15th, 1859, and in *Les Poètes Français*, 1862.

CXVI. Thought by Jacques Crépet (*op. cit.*) to have been inspired by a passage in Hoffmann's *Posthumous Tales*, of which a translation was published by Champfleury in 1856. First published in *L'Artiste*, October 15th, 1860.

CXVII. First published in *L'Artiste*, October 15th, 1860.

CXVIII. Composed in 1859. Published in *La Causerie*, January 22nd, 1860, and in *L'Almanach parisien*, 1861.

CXIX. First published in *La Semaine Théâtrale*, February 1st, 1852.

CXXI. Inspired by a statue by Ernest Christophe exhibited in the Salon of 1859. First published in *La Revue Contemporaine*, March 15th, 1859.

CXXII. First published in *La Revue Contemporaine*, May 15th, 1860.

CXXIII. Composed, according to Prarond, before 1844. Baudelaire, in a letter to his mother, remarks that this poem and *La servante au grand cœur* (CXXIV) refer to their old life together and that he purposely left them without titles or notes because he had a horror of prostituting the intimate details of family life. The house described was at Neuilly, and the servant was Mariette, to whom Baudelaire was devoted.

CXXIV. See note on CXXIII.

CXXVI. First published in *La Revue Contemporaine*, May 15th, 1860.

CXXVII. Composed, according to Prarond, before the end of 1843, when Baudelaire was still living with his mother and his stepfather, General Aupick. First published in *La Semaine Théâtrale*, February 1st, 1852.

CXXVIII. Composed, according to Prarond, before the end of 1843. First published under the title *Le Vin des Honnétes Gens*, in *Le Musée des Familles*, June, 1850.

CXXIX. Composed, according to Prarond, before 1844, but much reworked.

CXXX. Composed, according to Prarond, before the end of 1843, and inspired by an incident in *Champavert* by Petrus Borel. The poem was put to music by Villiers de l'Isle-Adam, who used to sing it at literary banquets. First published in *L'Echo des Marchands de Vins*, 1848.

CXXXIII. Published in *La Revue européenne*, September 15th, 1861, in *Le Boulevard*, January 12th, 1862, and in *Le Parnasse contemporain*, 1866.

CXXXIV. First published under the title *La Volupté* in *La Revue des Deux-Mondes*, June 1st, 1855.

CXXXV. The "unknown master" is unidentified and, perhaps, imaginary.

CXXXIX. Composed, according to Prarond, before the end of 1843.

CXL. Probably inspired, or provoked, by Jeanne Duval. First published in *La Revue des Deux-Mondes*, June 1st, 1855.

CXLI. Inspired by a passage in Gérard de Nerval's *Voyage à Cythère*. First published in *La Revue des Deux-Mondes*, June 1st, 1855.

CXLII. Said by A. Van Bever (*Fleurs du Mal*, 1917) to have been inspired by two engravings by Hendrik Goltzius (1558-1616). The two engravings in question represent amorini blowing bubbles, and in one case seated upon, and in the other resting on, a skull. Baudelaire would seem to have been inspired by the former of these only. First published in *La Revue des Deux-Mondes*, June 1st, 1855.

CXLIII. First published in *La Revue de Paris*, October, 1852. The mother of the poet objected strongly to the inclusion of this poem in the posthumous edition, but Asselineau threatened that both he and Banville would abandon the whole project if she insisted on its suppression.

CXLVI. This poem was set to music by Villiers de l'Isle-Adam. First published in *Le Messager de l'Assemblée*, April 9th, 1851.

CXLVII. This poem was set to music by Maurice Rollinat.

CXLVIII. First published in *Le Messager de l'Assemblée*, April 9th, 1851, but almost entirely altered later.

CXLIX. A slightly different version was published by *La Revue du XIXe siècle*, January 1st, 1867.

CL. Dedicated to Felix Nadar, and given to him March 12th, 1860. First published in *La Revue Contemporaine*, May 15th, 1860.

CLI. First published in *La Revue Française*, April 10th, 1859. In the last stanza of Part VI of this poem, the first line is the editor's version, replacing a misreading by Mr. Huneker. In Part VII, Huneker's version lacks the last stanza; Miss Millay's translation of it reads:

> We know this ghost—those accents!—Pylades! comforter
> And friend!—his arms outstretched!—ah, and this ghost we know,
> That calls, 'I am Electra! Come!'—the voice of her
> Whose lost, belovèd knees we kissed so long ago.

CLII. One of the poems suppressed by the legal judgment of August 20th, 1857.

CLIII. One of the poems suppressed by the legal judgment of August 20th, 1857.

CLIV. Inspired by Madame Sabatier, and sent to her in a disguised hand, December 9th, 1852. Suppressed by the legal judgment of August 20th, 1857.

CLV. First published in *Les Poètes de l'Amour*, 1850. Poem suppressed by the judgment of August 20th, 1857.

CLVI. Poem suppressed by the judgment of August 20th, 1857.

CLVII. Poem suppressed by the judgment of August 20th, 1857.

CLVIII. Probably inspired by Jeanne Duval. Not included in the 1868 edition.

CLIX. A manuscript of this poem has survived and was reproduced in facsimile in *Le Manuscrit Autographie*, 1927.

CLX. Amina Boschetti, the dancer and pupil of Taglioni, made her debut at the Théâtre de la Monnaise, Brussels, in September, 1864.

CLXI. A manuscript of this poem has survived and is reproduced in facsimile in *Les Fleurs du Mal.* Fasquelle, Paris, 1917.

CLXII. The irony of these verses is that M. Monselet, a friend of Baudelaire, had reproached him for his choice of unpleasant images, preferring himself to see everything *couleur de rose*.